his old man just came in and had a heart attack. He scared me to death! I was the only one in the room—Harriet had gone to the ladies' room. I had to be with him until help came. He gave me—"

I stopped abruptly. *"No one,"* he had said, had insisted. *"Promise,"* he said. And I had.

Do I really owe him my silence? I asked myself. I don't even know him.

But you don't know this sandy-haired, heavy-browed man standing beside you either, I answered myself. You only met him an hour or so ago. You mustn't bleed on him anymore.

"He gave me quite a scare," I said, my decision made. I laughed awkwardly. "I'm not used to anything more complicated than the common cold or one of my students throwing up."

But what do I do if he dies?

I fretted about this all the way home until the sight of the Zooks' large two-story farmhouse brought a smile in spite of my worries. I climbed out of the car, caught again in the glory and magic of actually being on an Amish farm. Then I slid my hands in the pockets of my Bermudas and felt the key.

My smile faded.

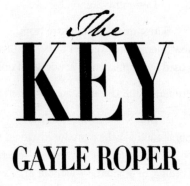

The KEY

GAYLE ROPER

PALISADES

This is a work of fiction. The characters, incidents, and dialogues are
products of the author's imagination and are not to be
construed as real. Any resemblance to actual events or persons,
living or dead, is entirely coincidental.

THE KEY
published by Palisades
a division of Multnomah Publishers, Inc.

and in association with the literary agency of Sara A. Fortenberry

©1998 by Gayle Roper
International Standard Book Number: 1-57673-223-1

Cover illustration by Heidi Oberheide
Design by Brenda McGee

Scripture quotations are from:
The Holy Bible, New International Version © 1973, 1984 by International
Bible Society, used by permission of Zondervan Publishing House

Printed in the United States of America

Library of Congress Cataloging-in-Publication Data:
Roper, Gayle G.
The key / by Gayle Roper.
        p. cm.   ISBN 1-57673-223-1 (alk. paper)
    I. Title.
PS3568.O68K48   1998   97-37109
813'.54—dc21   CIP

98 99 00 01 02 03 04 — 10 9 8 7 6 5 4 3 2 1

In loving memory of
Shirley A. Eaby
sister in the Lord
writing buddy
special friend

I have set before you life and death, blessings and curses.
Now choose life, so that you and your children may live
and that you may love the LORD your God,
listen to his voice, and hold fast to him.

DEUTERONOMY 30:19–20

ONE

By the time Jon Clarke What's-his-name drove me to the hospital, my terrible inner trembling had stopped. My hands were still cold, and the towel pressed to my cheek was still sopping up blood, but I felt almost in control again. Now if I could only stop shaking, I'd be fine.

I'd been so sure I'd lost my face…my stomach still curdled at the memory. All I had done was bend down to pet Hawk, the sable-and-tan German shepherd sleeping contentedly in the late August sun. I didn't know he had a nasty barbed-wire cut hiding under that sleek, hot fur.

I was horrified when he lashed out, startled by the pain, and got me in the cheek. I don't know about the dog, but what exquisite relief I felt when I realized that he hadn't actually bitten me, just caught my face with a fang. Just the thought of what would have happened if he'd closed his mouth made me break out in a fine sweat.

How dumb to touch a sleeping dog, I thought as I rearranged my towel to find an area not yet stained with blood. Dumb, dumb, dumb.

"You don't have to wait," I said to Jon Clarke. He was sitting quietly beside me in a bright orange plastic chair in the otherwise empty emergency room, his long legs stretched out before him, the picture of long-suffering and quiet accommodation. It didn't matter how much time things took; clearly he was prepared to be gallant and wait it out.

"Really," I said. "I'll be all right. You can go."

I was embarrassed to have inflicted myself upon this man I didn't know, this man whose last name I couldn't even remember. He'd pulled into the Zooks' drive just as I bent over the dog. While everyone else overreacted to my accident—Jake Zook yelling at the innocent dog, Mary plying me with towels and bemoaning my possible disfigurement—this stranger, Jon Clarke Something-or-other, had silently and swiftly put me into his car and driven me here.

He smiled at me now. "Of course I'll wait for you. I'd never run out on a lady in distress. Besides, you'll need a way home."

"I could call a cab."

"Bird-in-Hand is too far from Lancaster for that. It would cost a fortune." He smiled at me again, politely patient. "It's better if I just wait."

I gritted my teeth. Just what I needed, a shining knight, when I was in no condition to play the lady. I smiled ungraciously and winced.

"Hurt much?"

Of course it hurt. What did he think? I didn't state the obvious.

"The strange thing is that my tongue can push into the wound from the inside of my mouth. Only a thin piece of skin on my inner cheek keeps the puncture from going all the way through." I pushed against my cheek with my tongue. It was a creepy sensation to feel that hole, but I couldn't resist doing it.

He looked properly impressed and apparently decided to keep talking to distract me from my pain and injury. I must say, he shouldered his burden with stoic determination and great charm.

"Have you lived in the Lancaster area long?" he asked, and I could have sworn he actually cared.

"Two years. I love it here."

"Were you at the Zooks' to visit Jake too?"

I shook my head. "I live there."

That stopped him. "Really? On the farm?" He raised an eyebrow at me, an improbably dark eyebrow considering the light brown of his hair. "How long have you been living there?"

I glanced at the clock on the wall. "About three hours."

The eyebrow rose once again. "You're kidding."

I shook my head glumly. "Great beginning, isn't it? Todd spent the morning and early afternoon helping me move, and he'd just left. I was on my way into the house when I stopped to pet Hawk." I sighed. "They'll probably decide I'm too much trouble to have around."

I pulled the towel from my cheek and studied the bloody patterns on the white terry cloth. They looked like abstract art. I was an artist myself, but I never painted compositions like this. I liked more realism.

Uptight and unimaginative, according to certain professors and students from my college days. "Flex!" they said. "Soar! Paint as your spirit leads." I flexed and soared with the best of them, but the finished work still looked like what it was.

I refolded the towel, burying the modern art, then reapplied a clean area and pressed tightly.

"Who's Todd?" Jon Clarke asked.

I shrugged. Good question. "Todd Reasoner. A friend."

"Oh, I know him."

"You do?" As we talked, I poked my tongue into the hole in my cheek, not thinking.

"Don't do that," he ordered.

"Do what?"

"Don't push against your cheek like that. What if that thin piece of skin ruptures? Infection. Scarring. Who knows?"

I frowned. I wanted to tell him that I'd play with the inside of my cheek if I felt like it, but he was probably right. I didn't want to rupture that thin covering so delicately protecting the inside of my mouth. And I certainly didn't want to do anything to encourage the possibility of scarring. I'd looked in the mirror enough to know that my face didn't need that kind of help.

"You're very fortunate, you know," he said, as if he hadn't just given me a little lecture. "Not many people get to stay on an Amish farm because of their closed society."

I nodded. "I do know. I consider this opportunity a gift straight from God. One day my principal mentioned that he had Amish friends who were willing to take in a boarder. I got the Zooks' name and contacted them right away."

I didn't tell him how I'd worn my only conservative clothes—a navy skirt and white blouse—when I'd gone to the farm the first time to meet the Zooks and discuss the rental possibilities. I hadn't been certain what unknown ethnic land mines I'd have to negotiate, so I determined to at least defuse the one I knew about.

To my delight, I'd found Mary and John Zook gracious, respectful, and kind. They might demand the simple life of themselves and their family, but it was immediately obvious that they would not expect the same of me.

"Your principal?" Jon Clarke said. "So you teach."

I nodded. "Elementary art."

"When I first pulled in the drive, I thought you must be lucky Jake's visiting nurse."

Lucky Jake? "Not me," I said. "I'd be a crummy nurse."

"But a good teacher."

"Adequate, anyway. And I get the summers off to study and paint. How do you know the Zooks?"

"I've known them forever. My aunt and uncle live down the road from them. But I haven't seen them for several years. In fact, I haven't been to the Lancaster area for a long time."

So I'd bled all over his first visit in years. Great. "Was it a job that kept you away?"

"Schooling. I just finished my doctorate in counseling."

"Really?" I said, impressed.

"No, I confess; I'm lying. I just thought it sounded like a wonderful way to impress a pretty girl."

I looked at him strangely, and he smiled impudently back. "Really?" he said in a drop-dead imitation of me.

Flustered, I looked away from his laughing eyes and said, "I was just trying to make decent conversation."

His smile deepened—it was, I noticed, a most wonderful smile, crinkling his eyes almost shut and inviting me to smile along, which I was careful not to do because of my cheek— and he gave his head a little shake. "It's my strange sense of humor," he explained. "I take some getting used to."

"Kristina Matthews?" called the woman at the desk. Her nameplate said she was Harriet. She scanned the empty room as though there might be several Kristinas lurking about, and I resisted the urge to glance over my shoulder to see who had sneaked in while I talked with Jon Clarke.

When I stood, Harriet smiled brightly. "Right through here, please."

As I entered the treatment area, I passed a teenage boy staggering out on new crutches and a woman in a bathing suit with her arm in a fresh white cast. The walking wounded. What would my battle scars be?

Five minutes later I looked away as the nurse stabbed me expertly with a needle.

"This tetanus shot may cause your arm to swell or stiffen," she said sadly. As I listened, I couldn't decide whether her sorrow was because I might swell or because I might not. "If it swells or stiffens, don't worry. Take aspirin or Tylenol and call your personal physician if the pain persists." She turned away with another great sigh and began cleaning the treatment area.

I slid off the examination table and looked at my wobbly reflection in the glass doors of the supply cupboard. The white butterfly bandage stuck on the middle of my left cheek distorted my face slightly, but I didn't mind. There had been no need for stitches.

"Any scarring will be minimal," said the doctor absent-mindedly. He was a good match for the nurse. I doubt he even noticed her melancholia. "Just keep the wound dry and check with your regular doctor next week to have it redressed." He handed me a paper. "It tells you here. And you're certain the dog had his shots?"

I nodded, took the paper, and hurried to the waiting room. At least Jon Clarke hadn't had to wait too long.

But the waiting room was empty. My angel of mercy had flown the coop. I was standing there wondering what to do next when Harriet at the desk called to me.

"Don't worry, honey. He'll be right back. He said he just had to run an errand."

I nodded with disproportionate relief.

"Men," said Harriet sympathetically. "You never know what they're going to do, do you? Sometimes they just take off and you never see them again. But he said he was coming back." She shrugged philosophically. "He looked nice enough to me. I think you can trust him, don't you?" She got up from her desk. "I've got to get to the ladies' room. I'm talking emergency, believe me. Stay here by the desk and watch things for me, will you?"

I hesitated. "What if someone comes in?"

"Tell them I'll be back in a minute. But don't worry," she

called over her shoulder as she disappeared through a door. "Nothing big ever happens Saturday afternoon."

Taking no comfort in those words, I looked at the quiet waiting room.

No one, Lord, okay? Not until she gets back. Okay?

The thought had barely formed when the emergency door slid open and an older man in khaki work clothes entered. His face, damp with perspiration, matched the color of the white envelopes sticking out of his shirt pocket, and he was rubbing his left arm. He stopped beside me at the desk.

"I think I'm having a heart attack," he said conversationally, and I felt my own heart stop beating and my mouth go dry.

He staggered suddenly, and I reached out instinctively, taking his arm and lowering him into Harriet's chair.

"I'm sorry," he whispered.

"Don't apologize!" Now my heart was beating so loudly in my ears that I could barely hear myself talk. "Don't worry. Someone will be here to help you in a minute."

Suddenly he stopped kneading his arm and pressed his hand hard against his chest. His face contorted and I froze. He was going to die right here while Harriet was in the ladies' room!

After a minute he relaxed, and I began to breathe again. I ran to the door of the treatment area. "Help, somebody! Help!"

The sad-faced nurse leaned out of a curtained cubicle. "Is anyone bleeding?" she called, obviously distracted by what was happening behind the curtains. She didn't even look at me.

I shook my head. "No, but—"

"Then we'll be there as soon as we can." And she disappeared. I could see several pairs of feet below the curtain and hear several voices including that of my doctor barking orders with an impressive authority. Through a door down the hall I could see an ambulance with its back doors still open.

"But he needs you now," I called desperately. "He really does. It's his—"

"We'll be there in a minute!" she yelled just as a great cascade of blood flowed onto the floor.

Pushing down panic and not knowing what else to do, I went back to the man.

"They'll be here in a minute," I said with all the confidence I could muster.

"Had one before," he whispered to me. "Don't worry. It'll be all right. I'm not ready to die yet. I've got stuff to do."

I tried to smile encouragingly, but between my punctured cheek and my fear, I think it was more of a grimace. The man seemed to appreciate my effort anyway.

Dear God, I screamed in silent prayer, *where's Harriet? Send me some help! Fast! Please!*

"What's your name? Are you Harriet?" the man asked as he rested his head wearily against the wall.

I shook my head. "Kristie Matthews. Should you be talking?"

"I drove myself here. You don't think talking is any worse than that, do you?"

"You drove yourself here? With a heart attack?"

He smiled faintly. "I had to get here somehow, didn't I? And I didn't think you were Harriet. You don't look like a Harriet."

Suddenly he raised his head and looked at me intently. "Will you do me a favor, Kristie Matthews?"

I leaned close to hear his weak voice. "Of course."

"Keep this for me." He fumbled in his shirt pocket, reaching behind the envelopes. "But tell no one—*no one*—that you have it." He slipped a key into my cold hand and folded my fingers over it.

I heard a gasp behind me. Thank God, Harriet was back.

"Heart attack," I said, but Harriet was three steps ahead of me.

Her voice boomed over the P. A. "Dr. Michaels, Dr. Michaels, stat! Dr. Michaels, code!" Harriet disappeared back into the treatment area yelling, "Marie! Charles! Where are you? Get yourselves out here fast!"

An arthritic finger tapped my fist as it held the key, and I looked at the old man.

"Remember, tell no one," he managed to whisper. "Promise?"

"I promise."

He stared at my face as if searching my soul. He must have been satisfied by what he saw because his hand relaxed on mine and his eyes closed. "Don't forget. I'm counting on you," he whispered. "I'm counting on you."

Suddenly the room was alive with people. Doctors and nurses and orderlies converged on the sick man, and I stepped back with relief.

"Don't you ever go to the bathroom again," I hissed at Harriet who probably never would, not if she valued her job.

When the doors to the treatment area slid shut and I could no longer see the man, I collapsed in one of the orange chairs, struggling with tears.

This is ridiculous, I told myself. Why am I crying? I don't even know him!

I gave myself a shake and stared at the small piece of metal resting on my palm. Questions raced through my mind.

Why had he given his precious key to me, a total stranger? Why hadn't he let the hospital personnel keep it for him? Or asked them to hold it for a family member? What could it possibly open that no one must know of? And what in the world should I do with it?

It was a relief when Jon Clarke finally returned.

"I'm sorry," he said with that winning smile. "I got held up in traffic. I hope you didn't think I'd deserted you."

"Of course not," I said untruthfully as I slipped the key into my pocket. I hastened to correct my lie. "At least not after Harriet told me where you were."

He cocked that dark, heavy eyebrow at me again, saying as clearly as if he'd spoken aloud that he knew all too well what I'd thought.

I flushed and began talking rapidly. "This old man just came in and had a heart attack. He scared me to death! I was the only one in the room—Harriet had gone to the ladies' room. I had to be with him until help came. He gave me—"

I stopped abruptly. *"No one,"* he had said, had insisted. *"Promise,"* he said. And I had.

Do I really owe him my silence? I asked myself. I don't even know him.

But you don't know this sandy-haired, heavy-browed man standing beside you either, I answered myself. You only met him an hour or so ago. You mustn't bleed on him anymore.

"He gave me quite a scare," I said, my decision made. I laughed awkwardly. "I'm not used to anything more complicated than the common cold or one of my students throwing up."

But what do I do if he dies?

I fretted about this all the way home until the sight of the Zooks' large two-story farmhouse brought a smile in spite of my worries. I climbed out of the car, caught again in the glory and magic of actually being on an Amish farm. Then I slid my hands in the pockets of my Bermudas and felt the key.

My smile faded.

TWO

I'm fine," I assured Mary Zook when she hurried down the front walk to the car. "Really, I am. No stitches. Just this." I touched my cheek lightly. "And a tetanus shot."

She stared at my butterfly bandage unconvinced. "When I think of what would have happened if Hawk had closed his mouth." She shuddered. Her face was already made stern by the severe bun at the nape of her neck, covered with an organdy *kapp*. Now she looked clearly distressed.

"But he didn't close his mouth," I said. "And it wasn't his fault anyway. I should never have touched him like that."

Mary looked at Jon Clarke, and he nodded. "She's all right."

Suddenly she looked as if she might cry. Her eyebrows drew together, and she began to blink rapidly.

"Well, let's get you inside," she said as she turned abruptly and walked to the house. I heard a loud sniff and a clearing of her throat as I followed her, and I felt sad that I'd caused her this anxiety.

What, I thought again, if she decides she doesn't want me to stay here after all? If I'm stupid enough to get myself bitten within my first couple of hours, what else might I do? Burn the barn down? Scare the chickens so they won't lay? Blight the crops?

"Well, let me give you a glass of cold root beer before you go to your rooms," Mary said as we entered the house. "On a hot day like today you need something after all that you've been through. Going to the hospital's always scary, ain't? You, too, Jon Clarke."

I felt more hopeful. That didn't sound like a prelude to "I'm sorry, but…"

"Root beer sounds marvelous," I said, even though I'm a Coke person and all I really wanted was to go lie down.

"It does," agreed Jon Clarke. "I haven't had your root beer in ages. Why don't I get Jake?"

"I expect that's who you came to see in the first place," said Mary. "He's in his apartment."

He nodded and started for the front door, but Mary called, "No, you can get to him through there." She pointed to a door on the inside wall of the room. "Just knock. He's waiting, hoping you'd be back."

Jon Clarke knocked, and a deep voice called, "Come in."

As Jon Clarke disappeared through the door, Mary led me to a straight-backed chair at one end of what was obviously the relaxing section of the large room that filled the entire downstairs of the main house. A large hand-hooked rug covered the linoleum at my feet. I wondered if Mary herself had hooked it. Nearby, coal oil lamps sat on an end table and a bookcase.

I glanced curiously at the titles in the bookcase and saw mostly Bible study books, many in German, though there were a few lighter volumes. I was particularly surprised to see the brilliant crimson-and-gold cover of *It's Up To You* by Clarke Griffin. It was the very book I was reading.

At least we'll have something to talk about at meals, I thought in relief. I had spent a lot of time worrying about whether the Zooks and I would find enough in common to sustain conversation.

The other end of the big room was the working area and kitchen. Counters and a sink ran under the windows on the left wall, and a great wood-burning stove sat against the far wall by the back door. A large wooden table topped with an oilcloth filled the middle of the room, with a Coleman lantern and a Bible sitting in its center. A treadle sewing machine was tucked under a window on the right wall beside the propane-powered refrigerator from which Mary was taking mismatched bottles of dark liquid.

For all its spartan style, the room was welcoming, bright and airy with windows running on three sides. There were no curtains because curtains are worldly, but well-tended flowering plants graced the windowsills, and green shades hung from the frames.

A doorway beside the stove led to a one-story addition that housed the propane-fired water heater, the indoor plumbing, and the pantry.

Suddenly the front door burst open, and a young man exploded into the room, followed by a slight girl.

"See, Ruth?" said the young man. "I was right. I knew Mom'd be serving my root beer. Company's all the excuse she needs."

"And my pretzels," said Ruth, pointing to the plastic tub in Mary's arms.

"Hush, you two," said Mary with a smile as she pulled the lid off the pretzel tub. "Come meet Kristie."

It was obvious that the pair were brother and sister and Mary's children. All three had the same gray eyes and broad cheekbones.

"These are our two youngest, Ruth and Elam. Elam works here on the farm with John, and Ruth works in a pretzel factory. That's why she calls these her pretzels."

Mary turned to her daughter. "You're home early."

Ruth nodded. "Deacon Dan gave us the afternoon off."

Elam busied himself pouring root beer. He was a lean, compact man filled with nervous energy, the kind of individual who couldn't sit still, who probably relaxed by repairing things.

"Here, Mom, let me," said Ruth, taking the tub of pretzels from her mother. I smiled at her as she stopped shyly in front of me. What a wonderful painting she would make.

Despite her best efforts, little wisps of hair had worked themselves loose about her face and curled softly at her temples. Her brown dress, styled exactly like her mother's, was covered with a much worn, much darned tan apron. Her legs were bare, and, incongruously, she wore pink flip-flops with large plastic daisies over her toes. Her hands were strong; her nails were short. She looked all of ten years old, though I knew she was eighteen.

I took one of the fat, hard pretzels and bit gently so I wouldn't break a tooth. I was pleased when Ruth sat beside me.

"What do you do at the pretzel factory?" I asked.

"Make the pretzels."

"Really? Do you work a machine that pushes out the dough, or do you actually roll the dough and bend it into shape?" I knew they hand rolled and bent the pretzels at the Auntie Anne concessions located in malls and tourist areas from here to the Philadelphia Airport, but those were gourmet pretzels and priced accordingly.

"I roll and bend the dough," she said. "There are five of us who do it. Then Deacon Dan puts the raw pretzels in huge ovens to bake. It was the ovens that made it too hot to keep working today. It was so bad Rhoda Beiler almost fainted."

"No air conditioning?" I asked without thinking.

"No," said Ruth. "He's a *deacon*."

Of course. That explained the rolling and bending too. Machines wouldn't be acceptable. "Well, do you like your work?" I knew I'd find pretzel shaping old in no time. It wasn't as if you could be creative about their shape or anything. They couldn't be lightning bolts or flowers or clouds. Pretzel lovers are very traditional.

Ruth nodded. "I like it a lot. The girls I work with are all nice, and we can visit while we work."

Elam handed me a glass filled with a chilled, dark, slightly carbonated beverage, and I took a cautious sip.

"This is good!" I hoped my surprise wasn't too obvious. "I've never had homemade root beer before."

"I'm glad you like it," said Elam shyly. "I made it."

"You?" said Jon Clarke as he returned to the room. "I thought your mother was the root beer person."

"She was, once upon a time. Now it's me." Elam smiled and held out his hand. "It's good to see you again, Jon Clarke."

"It's good to be back, believe me," he said, taking Elam's hand. "And you." He grinned at Ruth and shook his head. "No more teasing the baby of the family. You've grown up very nicely."

Ruth turned a delicate shade of pink and hid her face in her glass.

I drank some more, too. I'd heard my grandfather talk about making root beer when he was a kid, especially the time it fermented and blew up all over the attic, but I didn't know that people still brewed it. It's too convenient to buy it at the supermarket.

"How do you make this?" I held out my glass.

Elam waved his hand vaguely. "You just mix root beer flavoring with sugar and yeast. The sugar and yeast work together, and you get carbonation."

"And alcohol, if you let it sit long enough," said Ruth.

"But we don't worry about that around here," said Elam. He

turned a mock-stern face to his mother. "Mom'd never let it sit long enough to ferment. In fact, she barely gives it time to carbonate."

Mary laughed at her son, obviously used to his gentle teasing.

"I'll take a glass," said a voice from behind me.

"Jake!" Mary started to rise and go to her son, then forced herself to sit and wait for him to come to her.

I looked with interest at the young man who propelled himself across the room in his wheelchair, noticing his strong shoulders and sad, lean face. When I'd originally come to the farm to talk about my rooms, which were on the second floor directly over Jake's, he'd been back at the rehabilitation center for a checkup. Ever since, I'd been both curious and apprehensive about meeting him. My experience with people in wheelchairs was almost nonexistent, and I wasn't sure what was expected of me or what I should offer. While the dog bite had provided our unorthodox and hurried introduction, I still knew nothing about him beyond his disability.

Elam quickly got a drink for his brother and topped off everyone's glass.

Jake looked at me. "Are you all right?"

I nodded as Elam and Ruth stared at me curiously.

"Hawk bit her," he explained to them. To me he said, "I'm so sorry. He's never done anything like that before."

"Please don't feel bad. It was my fault," I said again. "And I'm fine. I really am. No stitches or anything." Compared to your troubles, I couldn't help thinking, a dog bite is inconsequential.

"Well, Jon Clarke, are you home permanently?" asked Mary. I was grateful for the subject change.

Jon Clarke nodded. "I'm going to open an office and establish a practice in Lancaster."

"To teach people what the Bible says?"

"To teach people how to apply what the Bible says, Mrs. Zook. To counsel people with problems and teach others how to counsel."

Mary shook her head. "I don't understand why people can't just read the Bible and figure out what to do all by themselves. Why do they need someone to tell them what it says? And why did you have to go to school all those years to learn what's written there in black and white?"

"Not everyone's as smart as you, Mom," said Jake with a smile. "Some people need help figuring it all out." It was obviously an old argument and aroused no one's real ire.

As the conversation swirled about me, I drank my root beer and munched my slightly stale pretzel. In spite of my butterfly bandage, I couldn't stop smiling. Here I was, sitting in the living room of a real Pennsylvania Dutch home, my hosts and landlords genuine Amish.

I was still smiling contentedly a few minutes later when I climbed the stairs to my two rooms, my home for the next year at least. I stopped in the doorway and surveyed my quarters with pleasure.

My living room was very attractive, even though the two overstuffed chairs didn't match and the end table had led a full life prior to becoming mine. The truth was that the room could have been as stark and ugly as an army barracks and I still would have loved it.

Sitting along one wall was a huge, scarred desk.

"John found this for you at an auction in Intercourse," Mary had told me earlier as she ran her hand across its scarred surface. "He said every teacher needs a desk to work on."

Now I looked at the battered piece of blond wood and remembered kindergarten and the frightening Miss Stangl who had sat behind just such a desk. I put a flourishing philodendron on the corner to make it look user-friendly. Next I set my African violets on the broad windowsill where they'd get just the right amount of sun. My parakeet, Big Bird, sat in his cage in the middle of the room, where I'd left him before Hawk reordered my day.

"You, my loudmouthed friend, can go here," I said as I put him beside the chair nearest the window. He squawked his approval.

In my bedroom, a patchwork quilt of royal blue and crimson calico squares covered the great sleigh bed, and a small, hand-braided rug rested on the floor beside it. The nightstand held a small lamp, and on the dresser by the window sat a vase filled with great magenta and white dahlias that Mary grew in the garden off to the side of the front yard. My clothes, at least some of them, hung neatly on the wall pegs to the right of the door.

"Where do I put these?" Todd had asked earlier today as he stood in the doorway with an armful of my dresses, blazers, and blouses. He scanned the room vainly for a closet.

"Right here," Mary said with surprise as she pointed to the very obvious pegs along the wall.

"Oh," Todd said and began putting the hangers on the little wooden dowels. It soon became more than apparent that the pegs weren't installed with the amount of clothes I owned in mind.

Oh boy, I thought. The cultural chasm. Their austerity and my abundance.

"*Himmel*," said Mary. "I'll get Elam to put up some more pegs. Maybe he can do it after dinner."

"Don't rush him," I said as I laid Todd's second armload over the back of one of the chairs.

"No, no. He'll do it as soon as he can. It's important you be happy here, ain't?"

She had smiled and I had smiled, and I was still smiling, warmed by the care Mary had taken with my rooms. They were on the second floor of the *grossdawdy haus*, or grand-daddy house. When John Zook's father had given up the main responsibility for the farm and passed it on to John, a wing had been added to the house with its own separate entrance and ample independence and privacy for the senior Zooks. John and his family had taken over the main house.

Mr. and Mrs. Zook Sr. had lived there for several years until they were killed two years ago in a buggy-automobile accident on Route 340 near Smoketown. Their vacant wing had been the perfect place for Jake to come home to after his accident, though he only used the first floor.

An interior door had been cut in the wall between the main house and the grossdawdy haus, providing ready access to both Jake's wing and my stairway to the second floor but without invading Jake's privacy.

Right now the only thing ruining the perfection of my cozy new home was all the clutter from my move.

Get to it, girl, I ordered. Finish cleaning up this chaotic mess. Then you can lie down.

Instead I wandered over to the window of my living room and stood looking out over the patchwork countryside. Mary's garden was directly below my window, and on this August Saturday it was filled with cucumbers, celery, squash, tomatoes, peppers, onions, and beans of all kinds—string, lima, and wax. Along the garden's edge grew a profusion of cyclamen petunias whose purpose was to discourage the rabbits by their smell. At one end bloomed the elegant collection of varied dahlias.

In the field beyond the house, two of the mighty farm horses pulled a flatbed wagon beside rows of ripening cattle corn. A man in a dark shirt and black trousers, a full dark beard, and a wide-brimmed straw hat stood balanced on the wagon as he directed his team. I knew it was John Zook, and I itched to grab my Instamatic and freeze the scene for painting some day.

Later, girl. Right now, you need to get to work!

I turned and surveyed the chaos. I slid my hands into my pockets as I contemplated what to do first. And my hand brushed the key.

As soon as I touched it, I saw the stricken face of the old man as clearly as if he were here with me. My breath caught and my heart lurched. I was flooded with guilt. How had I ever managed to forget him?

Dear God, I pray he's okay. I pray he recovers. Please take good care of him. And please don't let him die!

I carried his key into my bedroom and put it on my dresser. I stared at it, waiting for some brilliant and practical idea to appear to tell me how to deal with it.

All I got was an intense headache, so I moved my boxes from the bed and lay down for a short nap.

Just before I dropped off to sleep, I thought again how terrible I'd feel if the Zooks decided they didn't want an English girl living on their Amish farm after all. I didn't want to lose my special year, abort my Great Adventure when it had barely begun. I'd met with enough resistance to my plan as it was.

~~~~~~~~~~

It was a month ago that I told Todd about the Zooks.

"You're going to do what?" he bellowed in disbelief.

"I'm going to board at an Amish farm for a year. I've already met the family and worked out the details."

Todd stared openmouthed, and I knew he was hurt that I hadn't discussed it with him first.

"Why do you want to do a thing like that?" he asked, genuinely baffled. "You already have a nice apartment."

"So I can paint."

"So you can paint?" Todd was almost at a loss for words. "But you can paint here—"he indicated my apartment— "where it's warm and clean and it smells nice. If you must paint."

"Of course I 'must paint.'" I was aghast at his misapprehension of what was so important to me. "I'm a watercolorist, Todd. Watercolorists paint. The Country Shop has taken two of my pictures and will take some more when those sell." I shrugged. "It's not much, but it's a start."

I paused, hoping he'd say something reassuring like, "And I'm sure they'll sell very quickly." But he didn't. He seemed to feel that any encouragement would only make me more independent, and I was bad enough already.

"Painting is more than brush strokes and color and technique, you know. It's perception and passion. It's feelings and emotion and ambiance."

"Ambiance?"

I nodded. "I'm boarding on this farm because I want to get a better feel for Lancaster County so I can paint it more accurately. You know how this area intrigues me, especially its people."

"I know. I'm the one who helped teach you about them when you moved here from New Jersey two years ago."

"But it's not academic knowledge I'm talking about."

Todd just stared at me, baffled. "Why isn't teaching enough for you?" he asked. "You know you're good at it. You like the kids and they like you."

"Oh, I like teaching well enough, but I love painting. It's a compulsion." I looked at the kind, somber, slightly stodgy lawyer before me. "Every time I take a clean sheet of paper and begin to block out a scene, I thank God for the indescribable joy it gives me. Don't you feel the same way about practicing law…maybe when you deliver an especially good argument or win a case against the odds?"

He frowned. "No."

"No? You don't like being a lawyer?"

"Oh, I like it okay. I just don't understand all this feeling stuff, this 'indescribable joy' stuff."

Poor Todd. I took his hand. "Todd, I teach because I have to eat and pay the rent, but if I could live off my painting, I'd do it in an instant."

He shook his head. "There's no stability there."

"Tell me about it. But some things are worth risk, aren't they?"

He just looked at me. Risk was something he didn't comprehend. Teaching was an honorable, safe profession, especially for a woman. I should be satisfied with it, and the fact that I wasn't bothered him not a little.

"But painting is so solitary!" he said. "It puts you in your own private world." Which he obviously thought a bad place to be.

Todd tried every argument he could think of to talk me out of going to the farm. I could see his frustration that he could argue a case in court and persuade judge and jury with his fluency but he couldn't budge me.

To him it was another yellow car.

"You can't buy that, for goodness' sake!" he'd said when he saw my just-purchased vehicle. "It looks like a taxi cab!"

"Never! I know sunshine and lemon drops when I see them."

"Sunshine and lemon drops?"

And now my foolishness was taking me ten miles from Lancaster to Bird-in-Hand and some backwards farm.

"Why is an Amish family letting someone English board with them?" he asked testily.

I knew he meant English in the broad Lancaster County sense of my not being German or Dutch as in Pennsylvania German or Pennsylvania Dutch.

"Why are these people letting you live with them?" he repeated grouchily. "It's very uncharacteristic."

"Because they need the money."

He shook his head. "That doesn't make sense. The Amish are very self-sufficient. If any of them ever do need money, their community will give it to them."

"They have a son, Jake, who was paralyzed from the waist down in a motorcycle accident, and his care is very costly."

The incongruity of an Amishman in a motorcycle accident bothered neither Todd nor me. We were aware that Amish children, especially sons, often rebelled against the strict ordered life of their parents. Most times the rebellion ran its course, and the children returned to the teachings of the church. Sometimes the children remained "English" or "fancy" or "gay," terms used by the local Amish community to denote people who wore clothes with zippers and printed fabric, people who drove automobiles and used electricity taken from poles along the road, people like Todd and me.

Unfortunately, sometimes events intervened in a Plain son's

wild oat sowing, and rebellion became tragedy.

"But if you live with those folks, you won't have electricity and all the modern conveniences. No TV or telephone. No hot showers!"

"It won't be that bad," I said. "There's a coal-fired hot water heater in the shed off the kitchen, so there's plenty of hot water. And I'll just get a cellular phone."

"But what about electricity?"

"When Jake came home from the rehab center, Mr. and Mrs. Zook ran electricity into one wing of the house for him. He has a little apartment on the first floor, and since my rooms are directly over his, I have electricity, too. And surely I can survive without a TV if I need to."

Todd snorted, unimpressed. "But it's an election year."

"I do know how to read the newspapers, Todd," I said tartly. Did the man never know when enough was enough? I certainly hoped he harangued juries with more finesse than he used on me. "And I'm every bit as interested in Adam Hurlbert's candidacy for the U. S. Senate as you are."

"So you keep telling me. I know, I know, you even met him at Parents Night because his stepson goes to your school. Big deal. And stop trying to change the subject on me."

"Change the subject?" My voice squeaked with aggravation. "You're the one who brought up politics."

"I don't want to talk about Adam Hurlbert! I want to talk about your dumb farm. How old is this Jake person?"

"What?" For a man who valued orderly thinking, he was being uncharacteristically scattered.

"This Jake guy. How old is he?"

Shaking my head, I said, "In his midtwenties, I guess. About my age. I think the family has made all these liberal concessions like the phone and the electricity because they realize that he'll never be Plain again."

"Well, I don't like it," Todd said. "Next thing I know you'll be running around in black stockings, a pinned-together dress, and a kapp."

"Oh, come on, Todd! You're being ridiculous! The last thing I plan to do is become Amish."

"Famous last words." And he stared morosely at my empty portfolio case resting against the wall.

I shook my head, exasperated. "Listen, Todd. I'm moving to an Amish farm whether you like it or not." I said the last few words slowly and emphatically so he was sure to get the point. We might go out together, but he hadn't the right to call the shots in my life. "And I'd like your support instead of all this flack."

He ran his hand through his hair, something he did only when agitated. His tight brown curls, now ruffled, escaped the tight control he tried to exert over them and sproinged exuberantly and unprofessionally about his head. He hated his hair; I was jealous of it. My straight brown hair fell to chin length with nary a wave in sight.

"I'm not going to the farm to become Amish," I repeated, softened by his obvious distress. "I admire them for their courage to be different, but I don't agree with them. I see nothing sinful about electric stoves or cars or a short curly permanent."

Todd looked at me sadly, and I knew that I had failed again to be what he wanted me to be, whatever that was.

THREE

When I awoke from my posthospital nap, I felt refreshed and energetic, ready to attack the chore of settling in. My injury felt like a mere twinge. The Tylenol was working. I began unpacking boxes and suitcases, dumping the contents on the bed. Soon the cases were tucked under the bed, and the boxes were piled by the door for disposal. All I needed to do now was put everything into drawers.

Instead I began getting ready for my date with Todd.

As I rooted through the various piles looking for my makeup, my fancy sandals, and my flowing dress with the bright splashes of color, my eyes kept going to the key lying on my dresser. I was glad I hadn't discussed it with Jon Clarke, but surely Todd was different. After all, he was a lawyer. He'd know what my obligation to the old man was, wouldn't he? He'd know what I should do if the man died or was hospitalized for a long time or was comatose or had a stroke or…

I brushed on some rouge, trying not to get my bandage rosy.

But the old man hadn't died or had a stroke or gone into a coma yet. At least I didn't think so.

"Tell no one. Promise."

Just Todd.

"No one."

I sighed. I'd better just wait and see what happened. Maybe I should never say anything to anyone no matter what happened. Maybe my promise was like the privileged communication between a patient and a doctor or a penitent and a priest. Maybe I was trapped for the rest of my life with a little silver-colored albatross hanging around my neck.

Maybe I was being melodramatic.

I grabbed my cell phone and, after locating my phone book, called Lancaster General. I would find out how the man was so I wouldn't need to drive myself crazy with speculation.

"I'm looking for information about the man who came into emergency with a heart attack earlier today," I told the woman who answered.

"Name?" she asked in a clipped voice.

Feeling rather foolish, I said, "I'm sorry. I don't know his name."

There was a small silence. "Then how can I tell you how he is?" Her logic was as razor-edged as her tone of voice.

"Maybe you can find out his name for me?" I suggested hesitantly. She was as good as Todd at making me feel foolish.

"I can find out his name?" Her incredulity bubbled down the line. "Ma'am, you made the call."

I cleared my throat and forged on. "I don't think there could have been too many elderly men with heart attacks this afternoon. I was there when he came in, and I talked with him before they took him away. I just want to know if he survived and how he's doing."

A sigh floated down the wire. Obviously I wasn't making her job easy.

"Please," I said, with all the plaintive desperation I could muster. I stopped myself just before I sniffled pathetically. "It's very important to me."

She put me on hold forever, but she ultimately delivered.

"I think you are referring to Mr. Everett Geohagan. He came

in this afternoon and is now in Coronary Care. He is doing as well as can be expected."

"Which means?"

"I don't know, ma'am," she said. "Probably it means he's still alive."

"How about visitors?"

"Are you family?"

"A close friend," I said, hoping God wouldn't think I was stretching the truth too far.

"Only family," she pronounced with great authority, and I thought she sounded happy to make me sad. But she wasn't as unfeeling as I thought, because she added, "Why don't you call back tomorrow? Call the floor itself." And she gave me the number. "They'll give you a more thorough report, and they'll tell you if you qualify as a visitor."

"Thanks," I said, but she was already gone.

I punched the off button, lay the phone down, and wandered to the window. My stomach growled, and I realized that because of the bustle of moving, lunch had been only a package of Lance peanut butter malt crackers and a Coke. No wonder I was hungry.

From my window I saw Todd pull into the drive in his silver gray Taurus. Discrete and unpretentious, like Todd himself. Why the man chose to date me was a great mystery since I am neither discrete nor unpretentious. I'm sort of artsy-flashy, not as crazy as some artists, but far from conservative.

I hurried down to meet him and waved to Mary and Ruth, who were working in the kitchen as I went through the great room. I was more than happy to put thoughts of the key and the old man away for a while.

"Had enough yet, Kristie? Ready to leave here?" Todd greeted me as he leaned against his perfectly polished car.

"What?" I looked at him in surprise.

His eyes narrowed. "What happened to your cheek?"

My hand went to my face. "Nothing much. A dog bite. I'm fine."

"Are you sure?" He studied the bandage as if he could see through it to the damage beneath. "A dog bite sounds pretty serious to me."

"I'm fine," I said, pushing his hand away. "And it's not really a bite."

"Who did it? That mangy German shepherd?"

"Hawk is not mangy," I said defensively. "And it was my fault."

"Oh, sure. 'Come on, Hawk, bite!' Is that what you said?" He shook his head in disbelief. "I do not understand why you're so in love with this smelly place and everything about it. I truly don't."

I couldn't help but laugh. His nose was wrinkled in distaste, his nostrils pinched. I had to admit that the barn was a bit ripe in the shimmering heat, but I wasn't about to let him know I thought so. It sat, timeworn but sturdy, across the drive from where Todd was parked. Its large door was open, and out of its recesses tumbled a trio of calico kittens. They chased each other past Hawk, who lay sleeping in the sun once more.

In the fenced area beside the barn, two great farm horses stood sleepily beside each other, nose to tail, each one's tail swishing flies for the other. One of the beasts shied suddenly as a fly drew blood. He kicked his left rear hoof to remove the fly and sent a red hen squawking in panic.

"You'd think, Todd, that after living all thirty years of your life in Lancaster County, you'd be used to the barn smell by now."

He shook his head. "Not in the summer. In fact, I consider

car air conditioning the greatest invention since the wheel. I can close everything out."

I took a deep breath. "But everything includes the good things, too, like honeysuckle. Besides, manure means growth."

Todd frowned. "When I think of manure—which isn't often if I can help it—I think of many words, and growth isn't one of them. Offensive is, or disease-laden, or repugnant. I can't imagine anything worse than dealing with tons of the stuff each year as these farmers do."

"You can't have milk without manure," I said. "Same critter gives both."

"Don't remind me." He shuddered. "I'll have to start eating my cereal dry if I think about it too much."

I leaned against the car beside him, looking at the farm. "It's all so beautiful."

Todd followed my gaze without comprehension. "I wish you'd listen to me," he said again. "You won't like it here."

Suddenly overcome with the sheer magic of the farm and my future as part of it, I hugged myself with joy and began to sing: "Old MacDonald had a farm, ee-yi-ee-yi-o."

"Kristie!"

I stopped abruptly, trying to look contrite.

"When will you learn that you can't go around bursting into song every time you feel like it?" Todd looked around self-consciously, then sighed in relief when he saw that we were alone. "People will think you're strange."

I took a deep breath, forgot contrite, and looked him in the eye. "You don't like my yellow car. You don't like my farm. You don't like my painting. And you don't like my singing. Is there anything about me you do like?"

"Come on, Kristie. That's unfair." He was hurt. "You know I care for you very much."

I nodded. "Yeah, I know. So you keep saying. Though how you can like me when you don't like anything about me, I don't understand. Why, I bet you think this dress is gaudy."

Without answering, Todd pushed himself away from the car and went to the trunk. I made a discreet face at his back, but I had to agree with him; it was gaudy. That's why I liked it.

I remained where I was, staring dreamily at the large two-story farmhouse. It was painted the traditional white with dark green trim, and an open porch ran across the front. The far end of the porch was hung with a sturdy wisteria vine, its thick woody limbs showing through the slender green-gray leaves. A neatly mowed lawn shaded by a great sugar maple wrapped itself around the house.

I smiled hopefully at Todd, wanting him to share my pleasure in the beauty of the scene bathed in the golden light of an evening near summer's end.

Instead, as he straightened from inspecting the contents of his trunk, he said, "You know, it still isn't too late to change your mind."

I bent quickly to pet one of the calico kittens and hide my irritation. "Todd, let's not talk about it anymore."

After two years, I thought, we're like two people on opposite sides of a window. We see each other, we admire each other, but somehow we can't touch.

Todd nodded, resigned. "Just remember, when you're ready to leave, I'll be there to help you find another apartment. But since you insist on staying for the moment, I have a gift for you to make things more bearable."

He walked back to me, took me by the arm, and led me around the car so I could see into the trunk. There sat a TV with a big red ribbon tied around it.

"Todd! What in the world?"

"My peace offering," he said. "I've behaved like a boor about your move, and I'm sorry because it's made you unhappy with me. Please accept this with my apologies." He grinned. "Now you'll be able to fill your evenings and keep an eye on our favorite local pol, Hurlbert."

I pointed to the TV, appalled. "You can't do this."

Ignoring me, he bent, picked the set up, and staggered up the walk to the house. "I can never understand why they call these things portable," he wheezed. "I'll just take it up to your room."

"Don't, Todd," I said, grabbing at his arm. "Don't."

But he ignored me, knocking on the door with the TV itself. Mary came, opened the door, and watched blank faced as Todd labored across her living room and upstairs without so much as a hello. I heard him trip on the last step and waited apprehensively for the crash that by some miracle never came.

How terribly rude he must seem to her, I thought as I waited, embarrassed and uncomfortable. I knew that Todd didn't mean to give offense—he wasn't that kind of man—but that didn't change the fact that he had. He returned smiling happily, unaware of my distress, flicking a little wave at Mary and Ruth.

I walked back to the car quickly, and when we pulled out of the drive, I said sharply, "Whatever possessed you to bring me a TV?"

Todd looked at me in surprise. "I know you were uncertain about bringing one with you for fear of offending the Zooks, but I saw a TV through Jake's window earlier today, so I figured it was okay. I got you that portable on sale. It's little and won't take up much space. It gets a great picture." He grinned at me. "I know because I tried it out this afternoon."

"You can't go buying me TVs!" Aside from the embarrassment, the monetary size of the gift felt uncomfortably binding.

I much preferred a bouquet of cut flowers. When the flowers died, so did my need to feel grateful. "Besides, with Jake it's different. Surely you can see that."

Todd turned onto Route 340, heading toward Lancaster. "What's different?" he asked.

"Jake can have a TV because it's a settled issue between him and his parents." My voice was loud, even to my own ears. I tried to calm myself. "I've never even discussed it with them."

"You mean you need their permission to have a TV in your own rooms even though you aren't Amish and even though their son has one and even though you're paying rent?"

I nodded.

"But you have rights here too," he objected.

"It's not a matter of rights. It's a matter of courtesy."

We came on a buggy moving turtle-slow in the buggy lane, which was essentially a broad, macadamized shoulder. We zipped passed, and I wondered as always what it felt like to have the air currents from powerful cars, trucks, and tourist buses buffet you as you inched along in such a flimsy contraption. You had to be either incredibly brave or incredibly foolhardy to be on the road in those things.

Most roads in the area didn't have buggy lanes, and cars pulled out to pass whenever there was a break in the oncoming traffic. I liked the way the tires sang different tunes as they crossed and recrossed the worn patches down the center of each side of these roads, shallow gullies worn in the macadam by the hooves of numberless horses.

"And it's a matter of grace," I continued as we turned right at the light in Smoketown to avoid Lancaster City and the bypass with its heavy traffic.

"What's a matter of grace?" Todd asked. "I thought we were talking about a TV."

"We are. It's grace that lets John and Mary suffer Jake's TV in their house. It goes against their standards, but their love for him lets them accept it."

"You mean you think they'll let Jake have one and not you?"

"No."

Todd frowned. "You aren't making sense, Kristie."

"I know." I searched for words to adequately describe what I saw as John and Mary's great dilemma. "The Zooks live by a highly codified theological and legal system."

"I know," Todd said stiffly. "I've lived in Lancaster all my life."

"Then you admit they need a powerful reason to break it or bend it. And Jake's physical condition is that reason."

"So he can have a TV?"

"Right."

"And you can't?"

"Not without asking. After all, it's their home. I'm the outsider. I'm certain they won't force their system on me; they've been nothing but kindness itself. But they should be allowed to be gracious to their guest instead of being forced to live with another breach in their code."

"First a trickle, then the world rushes in like a flood," said Todd sarcastically. "One TV, two TVs, then live burlesque on the front porch."

"Todd!"

"Don't worry about their legal system, Kristie. Like any legal system ever devised, it's full of holes."

"Spoken like a lawyer." I sounded huffy and ill-tempered and sarcastic even to my own ears.

"Well, it's true. There are so many inconsistencies. Electricity from public utilities is sinful, but water-generated electricity isn't. Driving a car is sinful, but riding in one isn't.

Owning a vacuum cleaner is wrong, but using one for the woman you clean for isn't. Hypocrisy."

"Inconsistency, yes, but not willful hypocrisy." I was furious at Todd's unfeeling generalizations. "You're forgetting that the Zooks are only people trying to accommodate a tragedy to a very rigid and inflexible way of life."

"Well, if it's such a ridiculous way of life, why are you defending it?" Todd was almost shouting.

"I'm not defending the system! I'm defending the Zooks!"

"Why?" he roared.

"Because I like them!"

Silence reverberated like thunder through the car as we struggled for control.

I glared out the front window. A pair of open buggies came racing down the road toward us, each driven by a young Amishman of about sixteen, each boy wearing a bright blue scarf tied cowboy fashion about his neck. Even as I fumed at Todd, I wondered how they kept their hats on at such a reckless speed and where they had gotten their worldly scarves.

He cleared his throat as a prelude to speaking, and I looked away, out the side window.

"I'm sorry." He cleared his throat again. "I don't really feel that strongly about the Amish. In fact, though I think they're wrong, I actually admire their courage and tenacity. My real worry is you."

"Me?" Startled, I turned to him.

"You're taking this Amish stuff too seriously."

I looked at his profile, strong and sharp against the western light. "I told you I'm fine."

He nodded. "I know. It's just—" He stopped, frowned, and tried again. "I'm afraid of losing you." He looked at me, emotion naked on his face. He reached out to me.

I was moved and automatically extended my hand to take his. "Don't talk nonsense."

A tension within him resolved, and he relaxed. "I promise not to raise my voice again," he said, squeezing my hand. "I'll be good no matter how much I might disagree with you or how silly I think your point of view might be."

"Silly?" I pulled my hand away, and my frail calm fled. "Silly?" A switch flicked on in my head. "That's the trouble with you! I couldn't put my finger on it before, but now I know. You think I'm silly! You condescend to me. Because I sometimes disagree with you, you think my opinions are foolish! Because I like to paint and buy yellow cars and live on a farm, you think I'm an idiot!"

Todd blinked at my attack and shook his head like a punch-drunk fighter. "Don't you think you're overreacting just a bit?" he said. "I never called you an idiot or anything close to it."

"Yes. Yes, you did." I pointed an accusing finger at him. "Oh, not in those words, but you did."

"Come on, Kristie, don't be silly!"

"Aha!" With that final word, I fell silent, and we drove around Lancaster in brooding silence.

Well, I thought, we've finally touched.

FOUR

When we arrived at Alexander Bailey's, my favorite restaurant, Todd and I both behaved as if nothing had happened. With no difficulty whatsoever, we slid the glass barrier back between us as we ate a delicious meal of Caesar salad, steak *au poivre*, and baked Alaska.

Truth to tell, I was appalled about my behavior in the car. I never yell at people. I consider it undignified and the mark of a thoroughly undisciplined person. I might jump to conclusions, the mark of an imaginative, creative person. I might burst into song at the least suggestion, the sign of a culturally literate person. I might like flashy things like yellow cars and swirls of color, the mark of an *artiste*. But yell in public? Lower myself to that? No, no, a thousand times no.

My supervisor during my student-teaching days had recommended strongly that I not even consider teaching high school.

"You're too gentle and soft spoken," she said. "Too sweet and kind. They'd eat you alive."

I spent a long time trying to decide if she was really telling me I was wishy-washy and spineless before I decided she just meant I was quiet. Introspective. Deep. At least I hoped that was what she meant.

Todd and I stayed safely surface in our conversation all through dinner. He told me about a case he was working on, a nasty divorce where the parents were using the kids as pawns and both sets of grandparents were also seeking custody ("All the grandparents agree that the parents are unfit. Their own kids! Of course, that's all they agree on.").

I told him about my preparations for the coming school year, rhapsodizing at great length about my new bulletin boards ("I found the most wonderful marbleized paper for the background, and there's lots of room for the kids to display their work.").

He told me about his difficulty finding a car mechanic he was happy with ("The guy thought that just because I wore a suit to work I wouldn't recognize incompetence when I saw it.").

I talked about a new art-supply store I had discovered ("Brushes of all sizes and of such quality!"). I even regaled him with an expurgated version of my afternoon in the emergency ward ("I was so scared I could barely breathe!").

By the time we left the restaurant, I think we were both thoroughly bored. It was not one of our better evenings.

"Can we stop by the hospital so I can check on Mr. Geohagan?" I asked as I snapped my seat belt. I had to do something to redeem the time.

Todd turned to me with the key almost in the ignition. "Now?" He glanced at his watch and frowned. "We'll miss the movie."

"Now," I said. "There's just time before visiting hours end, and we'll still make the nine-thirty show."

"But it's Saturday night."

"What's that got to do with anything? People aren't allowed to get sick on Saturdays? Or to visit sick people on Saturdays?"

"Okay, okay," he said with a totally uncharacteristic lack of grace. "We'll stop. But please don't be long."

I glanced at my watch. "Don't worry. They'll kick me out soon."

I stopped at the circular desk in the lobby of Lancaster

General and, smiling as sweetly as I could, asked where Mr. Geohagan's room was.

The receptionist turned to her computer, pressed a few keys and said, "He's not allowed visitors except family. Are you family?"

"Just a very good friend." Oh dear, I thought. I've raised my level of relationship again.

"I'm sorry. No visitors."

"Please," I said, dropping my smile and looking as desperate as I actually felt. "If I can't talk with him, I need to talk with someone who can tell me how he's doing. I'm going crazy not knowing, and I've come all this way because I can't get any satisfaction over the phone."

Just then an announcement came over the loudspeaker. "Visiting hours are now over. Visiting hours are now over."

I looked at the receptionist and sighed deeply. "Well, can you at least tell me what room he's in? And the number of the nurses' station on his floor?"

She nodded and gave me the information I'd requested.

I turned toward the door, paused, glanced back over my shoulder and saw that she was already looking back at the book she had been reading. I spun around and walked as quickly as I could past her and toward the elevators. I kept waiting to hear her yell, "Lady, I told you no!"

But I got around the corner and onto the elevator without a problem. I hit the button for Mr. Geohagan's floor and held my breath until the door slid tightly shut without a security person appearing. When I exited, I followed the signs to the nurses' station.

A nurse was reading some reports, and I stood and waited until she became aware of me.

"May I help you?" she said. "Visiting hours are over."

I nodded. "I know. I'm looking for any information anyone can give me on Everett Geohagan."

"Family?" she asked.

I shook my head. "Friend. I just want to know how he is and if he can have visitors tomorrow."

She looked through her reports until she found what she wanted. "He's doing as well as can be expected."

"Yeah, I know that. But what does that mean?"

She smiled sympathetically. "He had a mild coronary. The next few days are critical, and we will watch him carefully to be certain nothing further happens. If nothing does, he'll be able to leave here soon."

I felt relieved. A mild coronary. That didn't sound too bad.

"If he's still doing well tomorrow, may I see him for a few minutes? I promise not to upset him."

"I'll leave a note asking his doctor. Call tomorrow before you come in." She put the report back. "I'm sorry. That's the best I can do."

I nodded. "Thanks. I appreciate your help."

I found Todd sitting in the car listening to a Phillies game. He was rapping his fingers against the wheel, obviously annoyed at the length of my visit—or was it at the Phillies and their usual lackluster performance? It was tough to be a fan of Philadelphia baseball.

"We missed the movie," he announced with the import of a president announcing, "We lost the war."

I shrugged. "So we'll see it next week."

He just looked at me. Todd was a man who didn't shift mental gears too easily. If you plan to see a movie, by George, that's what you're supposed to do. "Now what?" he asked.

"How about home?" I said brusquely. I was tired of the responsibility for ruining his life.

We rode the whole way to the farm in a sticky silence. If I put my mind to it, I could be just as stubborn and childish as he could…undoubtedly the mark of a petty person.

As we pulled into the driveway at the farm, our headlights illuminated Ruth and Elam seated in an open buggy, their horse impatiently shaking its head.

Todd pulled up beside them and stopped wheel to wheel with the buggy, and I rolled down my window.

"Are you coming or going?" I asked.

"There's a barn dance tonight at Jake Lapp's." Ruth's voice was excited. "Everybody's going to be there."

"Including you two, I assume."

"You've got that right."

"Have a good time!" I waved as they pulled onto the road.

"We will," called Elam, flicking the reins across the horse's rump.

They disappeared down the road, the soft jingling of the bridle mingling with the muted rattle of bottles.

"Beer," said Todd critically. "Hear that? He's got a case of beer in the back of the buggy."

"I'm still amazed at Amish dating customs," I said, momentarily forgetting how miffed I was at him. "Unchaperoned dances, drinking, smoking, pairing off in the darkness. Our pastor would have a fit if his young people acted that way, but the Amish elders seem to accept it—or at least put up with it."

Todd shrugged. "This kind of dating encourages early marriage, and the sooner they marry, the less likely they are to leave the group. A single person might risk being shunned, but a married person has many more golden chains binding him to the church." He snorted. "Sort of like life insurance, only it's lifestyle insurance."

"That's a pretty snarly tone of voice," I snapped in a pretty snarly voice of my own.

"Oh, yeah?"

"Yeah."

We sat awkwardly as silence enveloped us again. Such tension was so unusual between us that I wasn't certain how to deal with it. Todd appeared as confused about appropriate quarreling behavior as I was.

"Well, good night," I finally said, for want of anything else, and climbed out of the car.

"Um," he said eloquently, climbing out and stalking up the walk after me. He bent to kiss me good night, and I turned my head, offering only my cheek.

"What?" he said in a steely voice. "I'm supposed to kiss it and make it better?"

That's when I realized I'd raised my bandage to him. "Very funny." I sniffed and let myself into the darkened house without a good-bye of any kind. It was a relief to be alone.

I went upstairs quietly, taking care not to disturb Mary and John, who had already turned in for the night. I got ready for bed slowly, weighed down not only by the humid August heat but by my thoughts about life and its complications. I hated it when I started thinking before I fell asleep. It guaranteed a restless night and a relentless morning headache.

Here I am, I thought, twenty-five years old, twenty-six in November. For two years I've been dating one man. At my age, that often means marriage. Mom and Dad certainly hope so.

"Not yet, Kristie? But he's so nice and handsome, and a lawyer besides."

"Not yet, Mom. Be patient."

I climbed into bed and plumped the pillows behind me. I took a pencil and a piece of paper. I titled the page TODD: GOOD QUALITIES. It didn't take me long to make an impressive list.

1. fine Christian
2. good lawyer
3. good salary
4. active at church
5. handsome
6. intelligent
7. loves me

I stopped and bit the eraser off the pencil. I spit it out and grabbed another piece of paper.

TODD: BAD QUALITIES

1. thinks my ideas and preferences are dumb
2. and me too
3. has no sense of humor

I placed the two lists side by side.

Dear Lord, do seven good qualities mitigate the force of three bad ones?

And what would Todd say if I told him about the key? I could just imagine it.

"What? You took a key from a man you've never seen before in your life, making a promise with who knows what implications? Who was this man, Kristie? Why'd he give you the key? Was he setting you up for something? What are you supposed to do with it? What if he dies?"

He would run his hand through his hair the way he always does when he's upset. *"Kristie, you should have thought!"*

It's terrible when you can't even win a mental argument with someone.

I snapped off the light and slid down on my pillow. Well, I

might not have been thinking when I took the key, but I was thinking now. Too much.

I woke to the rattle of a buggy and the clopping of hooves. I glanced at the luminous dial of my clock radio. Three A.M. Ruth and Elam were home.

Almost immediately I heard a second buggy pull into the drive.

Aha! Someone other than Elam was bringing Ruth home. Curious, I went to my window, but I couldn't see anything because of the jutting of the ell.

Well, Ruth, whoever he is, I hope your romance is running more smoothly than mine! Of course, that wouldn't be hard.

I fell back into a fitful sleep only to waken at dawn. I lay in bed with the predicted headache and listened to the morning farm noises. John and Elam would be in the barn feeding the animals and milking the cows, the extent of their Sunday labors. Mary and Ruth would be fixing a simple breakfast after which the family would go to church, scheduled today at Uncle Sam Zook's farm over toward Paradise. I smiled. Going to worship in Paradise.

I rolled over and tried to go back to sleep, but after a half hour of tossing and turning and muttering threats at myself, I finally admitted that I was awake for the day whether I liked it or not. I sighed and sat up. Then I took the Todd evaluations I'd written last night and stared at them.

Dear Lord, is it just pride that makes me feel unappreciated by Todd? After all, he can be very nice, and he has many fine qualities. Maybe after we're married, I can make him realize that he makes me feel stupid.

"Ha!" I said aloud. "Do you really think you could change a thirty-year-old lawyer who's as set in his ways as anyone you've ever met? Who are you kidding?"

Big Bird chirped at me happily. He loved having conversations.

"What do you think, Bird? I haven't got a chance, have I? It's Todd as he is or not at all."

Nodding his head vigorously, Big Bird sang.

I sighed and reached for *It's Up to You,* the book both the Zooks and I were reading. I found my place.

"The Holy Spirit woos us," Clarke Griffin wrote.

He draws us, convicts us, teaches us. But God in his wisdom seems to have left the privilege of final choice to us—and with this privilege comes the responsibility for our choices.

Sometimes we make mundane decisions—to floss or not to floss—and sometimes we make eternally significant ones—to believe or not to believe.

Many times we make wrong choices, and rather than accept accountability, we make excuses limited only by our imaginations.

"My parents always found fault with me. That's why I criticize my wife and kids."

"Everybody cheats on their taxes. Why shouldn't we?"

"Well, Billy started it!"

All these excuses for wrong behavior are just that—excuses, justifications for our falling short. It seems to me that as long as someone else is responsible for our troubles, we have no hope of solving our problems. If someone else consciously or unconsciously makes my choices for me, am I not well and truly trapped? Am I not hopeless?

"Choose for yourselves this day whom you will serve," Joshua said to each individual in Israel. He could not decide for the people even so proper a thing as worshiping God. Each had to choose alone and bear the responsibility for that choice.

The clopping of hooves caught my attention. The Zooks were leaving for church. I glanced at my clock. Seven-fifteen.

I climbed out of bed and watched the buggy out of sight. Did the Amish make fewer choices that I did? Or did they just make different ones? Or the same ones in different garb? Someone brought Ruth home last night. She had to make decisions about him, didn't she?

"And what decisions should I make?" I asked my reflection as I combed my hair.

I heard no answer.

FIVE

I loved the church I had found in Lancaster. The people there loved God, and it showed in their worship and in their genuine concern for each other. They had welcomed me from the beginning, and it was there I'd met Todd.

Today I found him waiting for me as usual when I came in the front door. I smiled wanly as he followed me down the aisle and sat beside me. Sitting together was a habit we'd fallen into, and I suddenly realized it probably meant a lot more to him than it did to me.

I turned sideways in my seat to put down my purse and Bible and was surprised to see Jon Clarke sitting behind me.

"Hello," he whispered, and I nodded my head in acknowledgment.

I turned back to the front, frowning. For some reason, I wasn't certain I wanted him sitting behind me. I had difficulty concentrating on the Scripture reading. I stumbled over the words of hymns I'd sung for years. Instead of worshiping, I wondered whether the back of my hair looked good. Or whether I had any tags showing at my neckline. Or whether Todd looked too possessive. Or whether Jon Clarke noticed I wasn't blood-spattered today. When the congregation stood for the benediction and the pastor said amen, I couldn't remember a word he'd said.

You're an idiot, I thought as I stood frozen in place, afraid Todd would turn to me, afraid Jon Clarke wouldn't. Just turn around and smile sweetly. Or bat your eyes, whatever that means, if it hurts to smile. Say something deep and significant like, "Nice service." No need to be as tongue-tied as a junior-high girl. Besides, you can't stand here like a pillar of salt forever.

I slanted my eyes for a quick peek at Todd and was relieved to see him greeting a couple on the other side of the aisle. I took a deep breath and turned self-consciously to pick up my things from the pew. I found Jon Clarke looking directly at me as if he'd been waiting for me to turn.

"So how's your cheek today?" His eyes under their improbably dark brows smiled.

My hand went to my bandage. "It's fine. I forget about it most of the time. Except when I smile."

"Then you mustn't smile." And he grinned so disarmingly that I automatically smiled back. I winced.

"Jon Clarke!" a voice called.

Jon Clarke raised his hand in salute to a man several pews in front of us, then turned back to me. "Are you free to get dinner with me somewhere?"

"Dinner?" I said intelligently, surprised and pleased.

"Or are you already busy?" He glanced at Todd.

I glanced at Todd too, still talking with his far neighbors. He was probably assuming we were going somewhere to eat because we usually did. But his comments and attitude of last night still rankled, and his assumption wasn't good enough. Besides, an invitation in the hand...

I turned to Jon Clarke. "No, I'm not busy. Not busy at all. I'd enjoy having dinner with you."

He nodded. "I may be a few minutes," he said as the man who'd hailed him a moment before approached us.

"No problem," I assured him.

As he slowly made his way through the crowd, shaking hands as he went, I slid out of my pew at the end away from

Todd. I was almost in the narthex when I felt a tap on my shoulder.

"Where do you think you're going in such a hurry?" Todd asked, but with a smile to show he meant nothing I could interpret as criticism. "I expected you to wait for me."

I shrugged.

"Well, where shall we eat?" he asked. "What are you hungry for?"

I shook my head. "I can't go with you today."

"Why not?"

I smiled sweetly.

When it became obvious that I wasn't going to tell him, he cleared his throat. "Look, you're not still mad at me about last night, are you?"

"It wasn't one of your finer moments," I said. "Or one of mine, for that matter. And, no, I'm not mad."

"Good," he said, relief evident in his face. "Then let's go." He put his hand in the small of my back to guide me to the door.

"I just said that I can't, Todd. I wasn't playing games. I really do have other plans."

He stared, obviously startled that I'd made plans that didn't include him. "But, Kristie—"

"If you'll excuse me?" And I walked to the ladies' room. I hung around in there for fifteen minutes, and when I finally peeked out, I was relieved to see that Todd had gone and Jon Clarke was still talking to people. I sat on a bench in the narthex and waited.

Finally Jon Clarke joined me.

"I'm sorry." He took my elbow as we walked. "As I told you yesterday, I've been away for five years, and there are so many people to see."

"So this is your home church?"

"As close to a home church as I've ever had. I've come here off and on since I was a kid. My aunt and uncle brought me along whenever I visited—which included my junior and senior years in high-school. I lived with them while my folks were in Brazil on an engineering job."

"You were away from your parents for two whole years?"

"Yeah." He shrugged. "We all survived. I didn't want to finish my high school career in Brazil, so I stayed here with Uncle Bud and Aunt Betty Lou. Nobody forced me or anything."

"I feel better," I said. "I had visions of Indy and Mrs. Jones leaving their kid behind while they sought adventure."

He laughed. "It wasn't like that. And being here was good for me spiritually. Since Mom and Dad sort of ignore God, this is where I heard anything of spiritual substance."

I thought about my parents, who were absolutely committed to God.

"I also came here regularly when I went to Lancaster Bible College," he continued. "And I was youth pastor here for a couple of years before I went to seminary and graduate school."

"Well, no wonder everyone knows you. Where's your real home—where your family's from, I mean?"

"New York City—at least for most of my growing up. That's why Mom and Dad always sent me to Lancaster County for the summer. They live in the mountains of South Carolina now."

"East side, west side, all around the town," I sang, before I realized what I was doing.

Jon Clarke looked at me and laughed.

I flushed and realized Todd was right. It was a stupid habit.

We stopped beside Jon Clarke's car.

"What about my car?" I asked. "Shall I follow you wherever we're going?"

"Let's just leave it," he said. "We can come back and get it later."

I looked at my car, and he turned to look too.

"Does it really look like a taxi cab?" I asked.

"Only if you're very conventional and yellow means cabs, not sunshine, bananas, and buttercups."

I smiled happily. What an insightful man.

Since many of the finest restaurants in the Lancaster area are owned by Mennonites, they are closed on Sundays. We decided to try Harvest Drive between Intercourse and Bird-in-Hand.

After we had visited the buffet, where I ordered an omelet, I leaned back in my seat. "Where are you living, Jon Clarke? At your aunt and uncle's?"

He looked slightly pained. "Do me a favor? Call me Clarke. My mother's a displaced Southerner, and she has the Southerners' love for double names. I don't."

"Why not just Jon then?"

"My father's named Jon, and two Jons would be confusing, so I use Clarke. But Aunt Betty Lou always uses the whole thing, just like Mom. People around here followed her example."

"What's your mother's name?" I asked, curious.

"Lucy Belle."

"Oh, dear."

"That's nothing. I have an aunt named Charlotte Mabel, who's called Lottie Mae, and another called Dolly Belle. Anyway, I sign my name J. Clarke Griffin."

Griffin, I thought as I buttered a piece of roll. Don't forget that. "Reverend J. Clarke Griffin?"

"Dr. J. Clarke Griffin."

"That's right. Graduate school. I forgot. Well, it sounds fine. It also sounds familiar, though I can't imagine why."

"It sounds strange to me. Too new. I imagine I'll get used to it at the college though."

"You're teaching?"

"Just like you."

I was surprised—and impressed—that he remembered. "Hardly on the same level."

"Oh, I don't know about that. Good teaching is good teaching, whatever the level."

"I can't argue with a truism like that." My cheese and onion omelet arrived, fragrant and steaming. I took the first delicious bite and thought midchew what a bad choice onions had been for a first date. Well, not a date exactly. Maybe a first conversation? a first afternoon? a first meal?

Didn't I hear once that cooked onions don't taint your breath like raw ones? I decided that I had heard such a thing and that it was true. I had to or I wouldn't be able to talk for the rest of the afternoon without putting my hand in front of my mouth.

I turned a bland face to Clarke and asked, "Where are you teaching?"

"At Lancaster Bible College, but just part-time. A class in practical Christian living and one in night school on pastoral counseling."

"Counseling's your field?"

"I'm opening a counseling center through the church. I like teaching, and it'll help me until I get established, but my heart's in counseling."

"Like me and painting and teaching."

"You're a painter? That's great."

"You sound like you actually mean it."

"Of course I do. Don't most people?"

I shook my head. "People tend to view it as a hobby at

best,or at worst, a waste of time."

"Are you good?"

I looked at him carefully and saw that he really wanted to know.

"Yes. I think I am. I may never qualify for the American Watercolor Society, but my work is good and constantly getting better. I have some paintings for sale at the Country Shop, and I'm talking with a couple of local galleries about handling some of my work."

Clarke nodded as he finished his shoofly pie.

"It's too bad it's so hard to make a living from things like writing and painting," he said as we rose to leave. "But there's no money in either unless you're famous."

Suddenly the nebulous wisp of recognition that had been bothering me took form. I stopped in the middle of the doorway and turned to face him.

"You!" I managed to say before he walked full into me.

The jolt caused me to lose my balance, and he grabbed me around the waist to keep me from falling. For a split second we leaned against each other. Then he let go of me, casual, smiling. He seemed much less affected by our collision than I was.

"Have you any pressing plans for this afternoon?" he asked as we got into the car.

I shook my head.

"Want to go for a train ride?"

"Strasburg Railroad? Our kindergarten class goes there every year. Are you really Clarke Griffin?"

"It's great fun for adults, too." He grinned at me. "Yes."

We were quiet as Clarke maneuvered onto the road. Then we both spoke at once.

"They forgot the *J.*"

"Do you know my book?"

We smiled at each other.

"You first," he said.

"They forgot the *J.* on the cover. It just says Clarke Griffin."

"So you do have my book," he said with satisfaction. He tried to be casual. "Do you like it?"

"Fortunately I can be completely honest and say yes. Of course, I'm only on page 32."

A little boy's smile when he gets the new red bicycle that he wants for his birthday had nothing on Clarke's. I leaned back and looked at him speculatively.

"What?" he said. "What?"

"*It's Up to You* is your first book, and it's recently been released. Am I right?"

"How did you know?"

"I recognize the symptoms. You're afraid to let your pride show for fear people will misinterpret it. You can't believe you've actually written something that people will pay money to read. You're afraid people won't like it. And you're concerned about being able to handle both the criticism and the praise."

He looked at me suspiciously. "Don't tell me you write too."

I shook my head. "It's just that I react that way whenever someone buys one of my paintings."

We looked at each other with pleased understanding as we pulled into the parking lot at the Strasburg Railroad.

The railroad runs through the Lancaster County countryside from Strasburg to Paradise. We found seats, and while we waited for the ride to begin, we watched a young family in the seat ahead of us. The two small boys wore engineers' hats, undoubtedly from the souvenir shop.

Suddenly the locomotive's whistle blew, and the younger boy grabbed his mother in a panic and collapsed against her in tears. She held him gently, smiling at her husband over the boy's head. Finally the train began to move, and the child's curiosity overcame his fear. He settled back in his mother's arms to enjoy the ride.

"Has your book sold well?" I asked.

"I don't know. It's a recent release, and it hasn't reached an accounting date yet."

"If it'll help, I'll run right out and buy another copy."

Clarke laughed. "And I'll buy one of your paintings."

"Bit of a financial difference," I said.

He shrugged. "It's only money."

"I've been working on the railroad," I sang. "Oops. I'm sorry."

"Do you often burst into song?"

"Regularly. It's one of my worst habits."

"As habits go, it's among the least offensive I've run into in a long time—and in my profession I run into some doozies."

The train puffed to a halt on a siding behind the lumber-yard in Paradise.

"The first lap of 'The Road to Paradise,'" said Clarke. "Now they'll move the engine from the front of the train to the back for the ride home."

I leaned out the window and watched with interest as the men worked. The engine was detached from the train and driven beside on a parallel track, steaming slowly past us.

"How will they turn the engine around?" I asked. "There's no turntable or anything."

"They don't turn it around."

"It goes all the way home backwards?"

"You don't think the engineer knows about reverse?"

"But backwards the whole way?"

"It's not like a car, you know. There's no traffic to deal with, and you don't have to worry that he'll jump the tracks." There was laughter in Clarke's voice, but no mockery or sarcasm.

I looked at him witheringly. "Of course he won't jump the tracks. Casey Jones would never do that."

"'Casey Jones, sitting at the lever,'" sang Clarke in a loud and sound baritone. The little boys in the seat ahead turned to stare.

I laughed. "The secret is in not singing too loudly."

After Clarke dropped me at church, I drove my buttercup car to Lancaster General. I nodded at the woman at the desk in the lobby, but I didn't stop. I didn't want to risk her telling me, "No visitors." I went up to the fourth floor, hoping that if I appeared assured enough, they would think I belonged there.

My stomach was queasy as I searched for Mr. Geohagan's room. I expected someone to grab me by the shoulders at any minute, a scary proposition for a rule keeper like me.

"And just what are you doing here?" this mean person would yell at me. "Get lost! And don't ever come back!"

But no one paid any attention to me even when I went into the room where Mr. Geohagan lay with tubes and wires fettering him to several machines. I was comforted by the steady patterns of the screens recording his heartbeat and other functions.

He lay in the bed with his eyes closed. His face was pale, there was a slight purplish discoloration about his lips, and he looked what my grandmother would have called "peak-ed."

Suddenly he sensed my presence, and his eyes snapped open.

I smiled. "Hello."

"Kristie Matthews," he said.

"You remember!" I was pleased.

"Of course I remember. How could I forget the girl who's been nice enough to call to see how I'm doing?"

"The first time I called, I had an awful time." I took the chair beside his bed and recounted my can-you-tell-me-about-the-man, which-man conversation. I felt like Abbot and Costello doing "Who's on First."

Mr. Geohagan smiled, and when I finished, his eyes moved to my cheek. "How's your dog bite?"

"It's going to be fine," I said, automatically reaching up to the bandage. "It's certainly nothing compared to your problem."

He emitted a burst of air, which I took to be a laugh. "My health is the least of my problems."

I blinked. It seemed to me that not much could be worse than some sort of coronary difficulty.

"But I don't want to talk about me," he said. "Tell me about you. What do you do?"

"For a living? I'm an elementary-school art teacher."

"Those children are very lucky to be taught by someone like you," he said kindly. "I know you're very good. You certainly took charge of me yesterday."

I thought about my near panic and shook my head. "It was all a front."

"Isn't that what teaching sometimes is? Acting like you're the authority when you're not certain you're even marginally qualified?"

"I think it's a lot more than that, but you're right about needing to be the authority. Kids need the structure that a firm-but-kind authority gives, though there are some kids who challenge you all the time." Kids like Nelson Carmody Hurlbert, stepson of the candidate for U. S. Senate.

"Tell me about your students."

And so I did, starting with dear Nelson himself. What I had feared would be an awkward visit passed quite easily. In too short a time Mr. Geohagan became visibly weary, and his breath came in little gasps.

"I mustn't wear you out," I said, rising.

"No one as delightful as you could do that."

I grinned at the gracious compliment. "By the way, here's your key." I held it out to him.

"Keep it," he wheezed genially. "I'll be here for a while yet. You just hold on to it until I need it again."

"Shouldn't I give it to your wife or someone in your family? Or someone here at the hospital?"

"No," he said quickly. "You are its keeper."

I frowned.

"Trust me. I know what I'm doing," he said, shaking a finger in my direction. "I'll tell you when I want it back."

"Okay." But I wasn't happy, and I didn't understand.

"By the way, would you be willing to mail a letter for me?" He turned toward his night table.

I saw a couple of business envelopes resting there and recalled seeing them in his pocket yesterday. I reached quickly for the top one to save him the movement. "This one?"

I glanced at it and saw the addressee was Adam Hurlbert. "Hey, he's my favorite candidate, too. That Nelson kid I was talking about is his stepson."

He nodded. "I'm afraid it needs a stamp."

"No problem," I assured him. "I just bought a book of stamps the other day. In fact, they're still in my purse. I'll mail it on my way home. And if there's anything else I can do for you, just ask."

"Thanks." He fell back on his pillows exhausted, and I left

quickly. I dug out a stamp and posted the letter at the strip mall in Smoketown on my way home.

SIX

I set my easel by the boll of the great sugar maple in the front yard, its massive canopy providing protection from the strong early-September sun. My bag with its brushes, paints, pencils, paper towels, and assorted paraphernalia rested against the leg of my collapsible stool.

I took a large sheet of composition board and placed it on my easel. Then I taped a piece of heavily textured paper to it, working flat as watercolorists do. I hummed to myself as I took a plastic bottle from my supply bag and went into the farmhouse to fill it with water.

I had decided that the Zooks' barn with its dilapidated grace would be the subject of my painting. I would put the cornfields in the background and some red hens and Hawk in the foreground against the great maw of the barn's door.

With clear water I wet what would become the sky, keeping the paper dry where I wanted the clouds to be. I applied a blue wash to the dampened areas, and when it began to dry, I softened the edges of the clouds with more clear water. A touch of gray wash on the undersides of the clouds gave them dimension. The cornfields with their green stalks and golden tassels came next as I worked background to foreground.

As these paints dried, I mixed cadmium red and burnt sienna for the barn and Prussian blue and burnt sienna for the gaping door. As always when I painted, I was totally absorbed and completely contented. I lost all track of time.

Finally I leaned back to survey my work. I was especially

pleased with the way the white of the paper was visible in a fine corona around the red hens, making them stand out against the deep gray of the door.

"Nice," said a voice behind me.

I started and spun around. On the walk watching me was Jake in his wheelchair.

"Do you always sneak up on people?" I asked, and it came out more brusquely than I intended.

"Sorry," he said. "I thought you were finished."

I looked at my painting again and nodded. "For the time being."

I rose and walked across the lawn, carrying my stool, and sat down by Jake. I looked from his wheelchair to the front porch and its four steps. "You must have a ramp someplace."

He nodded. "My entrance has one. Father and Elam built it for me."

"Then you can get around pretty well by yourself?"

"Sure. From here to the house and back." His voice dripped bitterness.

"I'm sorry," I said, flushing, mad at myself for making such a stupid comment and mad at him for making me feel so dumb. "That wasn't very tactful of me."

Jake sighed, holding up a hand apologetically. "It was no worse than my answer. I'm sorry too."

We smiled ruefully at each other.

I hated to admit it even to myself, but Jake scared me a bit. I'd never been around someone with such a raw, recent disability before. My own good health made his situation even more stark, and though I knew it was foolish, I felt guilty because of my functioning, albeit skinny, legs.

I took a deep breath. "Isn't it a beautiful day?" When in doubt about what to say, fall back on the weather.

Jake looked without enthusiasm at the sky, then at me. "Beautiful," he said in a flat voice.

"It or me?" I teased.

"What?" he said, missing the joke entirely.

I shook my head. The idea of trying to explain my cleverness was more than I could handle. We sat, silent again.

Strike two, I thought. I wanted to pick up my stool and go back to my painting, but I didn't see how I could. I searched my mind for something else to say, something that would not only get a nice, general, unemotional conversation started but also keep it going.

"What do you do to pass the time, Jake?" Before I could continue and ask if he had watched TV or worked at something with his hands or had read anything, seen anything, or done anything interesting recently, he answered. Or rather he reacted.

"What do I do?" he snorted. "What do you *think* I do? Nothing."

Strike three. I was doing about as well here as I had back in the old days in gym class. Or to mix metaphors, obviously talking to Jake was a minefield, and so far I'd detonated more than my share of emotional explosions.

I decided to brazen it out rather than apologize again. I saw that I could easily spend my whole time here saying I was sorry for some accidental comment or inadvertent hurt. Besides, truth to tell, maybe it wasn't my thick tongue but his thin skin that was the real problem.

"How did your accident happen?" I made my voice as matter-of-fact as I could.

"You sure you want to know?"

"If you want to tell."

He seemed to consider, and I waited for strike four. Apparently he decided to take the risk.

"Over on Route 10 south of Honey Brook, there are two steep hills," he said, his hands sketching a deep V.

"I know where you mean," I said, drawing the V too.

"Yeah?" He seemed to like that.

I nodded.

"Well," he said, "I was speeding down the first on my motorcycle last fall. October 20, to be exact. It was raining hard, but I was so busy picking up speed for the second hill that I never gave the wet leaves a thought."

I could picture him, crouched forward over the bike, hurtling down the steep incline, preparing for the long pull just ahead.

"As I neared the intersection at the bottom of the hill, a car ran the stop sign right in front of me. I braked and lost control on the leaves. I thought I was going to die. I skidded and flew off and finally came to a stop against a post. My back was broken when my bike landed on top of me."

His eyes lost focus as he looked into some private middle distance of memories and anguish.

I sat quietly, not daring to breathe.

Finally he blinked and looked at me. "It took less than a minute, a lot less, to change my life as I knew it. And the car never even slowed up."

"I'm sorry," I said inadequately. "I'm so sorry."

Jake smiled tightly and stared at his clenched fists. "Don't let it worry you. If I can stand all those months in the hospital and in rehab, I can survive anything."

We sat quietly again, Jake lost in his memories, I trying to grasp the enormity of his injury. This time there was no awkwardness between us.

He finally broke the silence. "You've been here almost a week. Do you regret moving here yet?"

I stared at him in surprise. He sounded just like Todd! "Why would I regret it? I love it here."

"Even with Hawk?"

My hand went to my cheek. The wound was healing nicely. "Hawk was just being a dog."

"You're not going to give in to the English habit of suing, are you?"

I laughed. "Of course not! It's not as though the dog did this with malice aforethought. And besides, I'd never do anything to hurt your parents. They're too nice. After all, I want to stay here, and I think that it will work better if I'm not facing you in court."

I looked over at the sleeping dog. "I think Hawk is wonderful." I threw my arms wide. "I think the farm is wonderful."

His eyes traced the barn, the fields visible behind it. "I complain a lot, but I love the farm too. Not farming, you understand, but the farm. The country. The quiet."

I nodded my agreement.

"Though sometimes," he said, sounding lost and small, "it's just too quiet."

Dear God, how do I respond to that?

Since I hadn't any idea, I changed the subject completely. "My biggest problem here on the farm is that my English inner clock just doesn't jive with your family's German one. I simply can't go to bed at nine or nine-thirty and expect to go to sleep. Nor can I wake up at five and expect to think."

"I know what you mean," said Jake. "I finally convinced Mom that I didn't want to get up that early either. It makes the day too long." This time there was no bitterness in his voice. He was merely stating a fact.

"I'm trying to persuade your mother not to stop her work to make me a late breakfast when I can very well do it myself," I said. "That way I'll be able to sleep as late as I want—at least for the next few days until school starts—and not feel too guilty and lazy."

"Good luck," Jake said.

"Well, I'm a guest, right? And how do you argue with your guests, even—or maybe especially—paying ones?"

"You don't know my mother well, do you?" said Jake skeptically. He waved at my painting, still sitting on the easel under the tree. "Is that kind of thing the reason you wanted to live here?"

I nodded. "I know it probably sounds pure corn to you, but I've fallen in love with Lancaster County. It's so beautiful and green and so culturally unique."

"It's kind of funny when you think about it," said Jake, "but I've spent the last ten years, since I was fifteen, trying to escape from this cultural thing you want to take on."

Now this was a conversation!

"Oh, no, I don't want to take anything on," I said, hastening to correct his misunderstanding. "I have too many problems with Amish beliefs. I just want to observe and enjoy and paint."

He shrugged, not quite with me. "Well, I guess you'll be all right as long as you keep painting barns."

"But not people?"

Jake shook his head. "The Old Order Amish like my parents don't believe in photographs. Or portraits. They see them as graven images. You know, 'Thou shalt not make any graven image or any likeness of any thing.'"

"I knew the Amish didn't like having their pictures taken, but I didn't realize there was a religious reason other than the fact that cameras are relatively modern. And, of course, they resent the invasion of their privacy by tourists who poke Polaroids in their faces."

I looked at my painting of the Zooks' barn.

"I'm not very good at portraits, and I prefer doing land-scapes, so I shouldn't have any problem. Still, I'd love to do your father's hands."

"His hands?"

"They're marvelous, Jake. Gnarled and strong, a farmer's hands. Do you think he'd let me photograph them sometime so I could paint them at my leisure? Do hands constitute graven images?"

"Who knows? Just don't ask him until he gets to know you. Then he'll realize you're not trying to use him. He's had enough criticism recently because he let me bring in electricity and a phone. He needs a period of rest."

"If people minded the telephone and the electricity, they must not approve of my being here."

Jake shrugged. "Probably not. Some of them are very con-servative and very touchy. They're afraid of anything new, any-thing that might be seen as a breach of community. But your being here's not as difficult for Father as it might have been because—" he paused for effect—"I'm really your landlord."

"You are?" I was startled, though the information made sense. I'd never quite figured out why John and Mary were willing to open their home to an outsider. They didn't need me or my money. I was only another complication in a life that already had more than its share.

But Jake as landlord made sense. And no wonder he was afraid I might dislike the farm. He didn't want to lose his ten-ant.

"The wing is mine," said Jake. "Since I don't use the top floor and probably never will, I decided to rent it out. I figured I wouldn't feel like such a charity case if I had some income. Father made all the arrangements with you because I wasn't home." He grinned impudently. "I think I'm going to like being a landlord, sitting idle as the money pours in."

I grinned back, but I was moved by how revealing his comments were.

"Anyway," Jake continued, "everybody knows Father's largely innocent concerning you, though people still gripe to him about me because I'm not Plain and I'm not willing to revert, in spite of the obvious chastisement of the Lord."

I was appalled. "Oh, Jake. Surely people don't believe your situation is God's punishment!"

Jake shrugged. "Some do; some don't. But let me tell you, I wouldn't blame him if it were true. I was one wild maniac. You wouldn't have liked me. In fact, you'd probably have been afraid of me."

I looked at the man in the chair, his shoulders strong beneath his knit shirt, his hands firm on the wheels, but his face nice. It was hard to imagine him as the man he was describing. "Maybe you're too hard on yourself."

"Maybe," he said. "But I doubt it. I put Mom and Father through all kinds of pain, but they always loved me. They don't seem to agree with those who think I'm being punished, but I do know they wish I were still Amish."

"Sure they do," I said. "I don't find that surprising. But shouldn't they be shunning you?" I had the typical English curiosity about this Amish teaching. "I mean, obviously they aren't, and I'm glad, but why not? You've certainly gone against the Order's teachings."

"You can only be shunned if you're a baptized member of the church, and that happens when you're around eighteen or twenty. That's when you place yourself under church discipline and rules."

I nodded, watching Hawk lope across the lawn and come

directly to me. He rested his chin on my lap. I put my hand lightly on his head and stroked. He closed his eyes in pleasure and didn't move.

Jake grinned. "He likes you. And he's sorry he hurt you."

"He probably doesn't even remember," I said. "Please. Tell me more about shunning."

"Everybody has to decide when they want to join church. My two older brothers, Andy and Zeke, decided not to join at all but to go fancy like me. My older sister Sarah decided to take the vow. She lives with her farmer husband, Abner, and their three and a half kids over near Honey Brook. Elam and Ruth have obviously chosen Plain too. What that means is that Andy, Zeke, and I have never been baptized; Sarah has, and Elam and Ruth plan to be."

"They haven't been baptized yet?"

"There's still a touch of *rumschpringes* there, though nothing like mine."

"Rumschpringes?"

"Rebellion. Sowing wild oats. All Amish kids do it in their teens. Then they give it all up and join church. I think Ruth and Elam are taking instruction now."

"So if Elam gets baptized, then changes his mind and buys himself a car and becomes liberal, he'd be shunned?"

Jake nodded.

"Do you know anyone who's been shunned?" I asked.

"Sure. David Stoltzfus from the farm across the way." Jake pointed across the cornfield. "He wanted to race cars, of all things. And my uncle."

"Your uncle?"

"My father's younger brother. He just couldn't accept all the teachings of the *Ordnung*, the Amish code of unwritten laws. He said he couldn't find them in the Bible. At twenty-two he broke with the church, saying he believed in salvation by grace, not works."

"And now none of you sees him? Ever?" Such an ostracizing was hard for me to imagine.

"It's not quite that bad," he said, smiling. "I see him. Or at least I did when I could get around. He lives in Lancaster, has a nice wife and a couple of kids. One's even named Amos, after Grandfather, but I don't think Grandfather and Grandmother ever saw Uncle Jake again after he was excommunicated. They couldn't understand his difficulty with what they considered the God-ordained way of life."

"Uncle Jake? Are you named for him?"

"Father has never admitted it, but I think so. I know Uncle Jake was his favorite brother."

"And they never see each other, your father and your uncle?"

"Once in a while Uncle Jake comes to visit, but it's hard for everybody. And he never stays for a meal. If he did, he'd have to eat at a separate table. It's too awkward."

"That's a sad story."

Jake smiled thinly. "In a way, being shunned is like being dead. If you're under the ban, people can't eat or do business or socialize with you. If you're married, your husband or wife can't have normal relations with you. It's a pretty brutal situation, and not many people can handle such total rejection by family and friends and community. But it's one way the Amish church keeps itself pure."

The screen door slammed, and Mary came outside. She waved at Jake and me and went to the garden to pick beans for supper. Hawk deserted me to follow her.

"Take Mom as an example of how the Amish think," said Jake. "She prays for me more and cries over me more because of my non-Amish status than because of my paralysis. She can no more understand me than Grandfather could understand Uncle Jake.

"But she and Father are realists. They didn't want the rift of excommunication in our generation of the family. That's why they didn't force us into the fold. Many of their friends disapprove, especially since Father's a preacher in the district. It's because of Andy and Zeke and me that he can never be a bishop."

I reached over and grabbed a little marmalade kitten as he ran past. I handed him to Jake. The animal spit and slashed the air with a tiny, clawed paw, then wiggled and squirmed until Jake let him go. Falling over himself in his haste to escape, he raced for the safety of the barn.

"I guess you could say that Father and Mom have bent tradition some," Jake said. "But they haven't actually broken the Ordnung. And our family's still intact."

I was impressed. While I had no difficulty understanding why Mary was more concerned about her son's spiritual welfare than his physical condition, I knew I had only the vaguest comprehension of the magnitude of the accommodations she and John were making to ensure family unity.

Jake laughed. "It's really funny on off-Sundays when there's no church."

"What do you mean?"

"Every other Sunday there's no service. Then Andy and Sally and their kids and Zeke and Patsy and their kids all drive up in their cars, and everybody climbs out in their jeans and Phillies T-shirts. Sally brings the ham she's just cooked in her microwave and Patsy has a Mrs. Smith's frozen pie still hot from her electric oven."

"Then Sarah and Abner pull up in their buggy, Amish to

their hooks and eyes, Sarah wearing her rimless glasses and carrying cheese and bread she baked Saturday because Sunday baking isn't allowed. The contrasts are a riot. It took Abner a while to get used to us."

I could just imagine. "I think it's wonderful that your parents have managed to keep you all together."

"It is. And you have no idea of the pressure some people put on them. If their Christian character weren't so consistent, I don't know what would happen in our district."

A buggy rattled by on the road, the driver a white-haired gentleman whose beard reached almost to his waist.

"It's Abraham, the patriarch," I said, enchanted. "Though I doubt Abraham wore a straw hat."

"With a brim three and a half inches wide, not a quarter of an inch wider or narrower," said Jake as he waved to the gentleman.

There was a barely perceptible nod in return.

"That's Nate Stoltzfus from over the way," he said. "He's one of the ones unhappy with my father, especially since he took such a strong stand with his own son David, the one who's the race-car driver."

I studied the old man with his set face, my imagination gripped by his story. Could a broken heart be hiding under his frosty exterior?

Jake stared after the old man, too, but with no pity.

"Dave Stoltzfus was one of my best friends, but I haven't heard a word from him since he left. It's like he wants no part of his past, even those of us who sympathized. Sometimes I read about him in the paper, and once I saw him race on *Wide World of Sports*."

Jake's voice became hard again. "They wanted him to confess before the congregation the sin of liking fast cars, but he wouldn't do it. All that terrible grief and pain, and for the life of me, I can't see the difference between Dave's gasoline-powered car and Nate's kerosene-powered motor on his well. It's that kind of hairsplitting that drives me wild! Dave says he refuses to be a Christian if he has to be so bound, and I agree with him completely!"

I was startled by Jake's vehemence.

"But I'm a Christian," I said, "and I'm not under any of those laws. It's not being Amish or keeping the Ordnung that makes a person a Christian. It's believing that Jesus died for your sins."

"You sound just like Jon Clarke." The way Jake said it, it wasn't a compliment. His dark, brooding scowl returned, and he said nothing for a few minutes.

Then, "Is that big, grumpy guy who helped you move in a permanent fixture? The one with the curly hair?" As a change of subject it was a bit heavy-handed, but I cooperated.

I shrugged. "He's a nice guy and all that, but we're—I'm—not committed."

Jake nodded. "The proverbial good friend?"

"And what's wrong with that?"

"Nothing. I've had a few 'good friends' of my own."

"Any special girl now?"

Jake's mouth twisted. "Are you kidding?"

Great. Back to square one. We're Banana Brain and the Prickly Pear, a truly dynamic duo.

But I no longer had the strength to deal with my indiscretions and Jake's touchiness. Excusing myself, I collected my supplies and prepared to visit Mr. Geohagan. Tomorrow he was having bypass surgery, and I wanted to see him before this new ordeal.

~ ~ ~ ~ ~

"You'll be fine," I told Mr. Geohagan a couple of hours later. "Bypass surgery is a common thing these days."

"Not on me, it's not." His jaw was clenched and his forehead furrowed. "I've got stuff to do. Important stuff. I can't stay sick!"

"Isn't that why you're having this surgery? So you won't stay sick?"

"I'm having it because some doctor wants to earn more money."

"Mr. Geohagan! What a terrible thing to say."

"Look," he said. "In case I don't make it, I wrote you a long letter about what to do with some of my belongings. I need someone I can trust to see that the right things happen, things that I've never mentioned in my will, never mentioned to anyone." He pointed in the direction of his bedside table. "The instructions are in the drawer." He stared at me through narrowed eyes. "Only read it if I die."

"Mr. Geohagan!"

"Just don't lose that key." He scowled at me.

"A lot of good it'll do me to keep it if I don't know what it opens," I said.

"It's written in my letter what you're to do with it if I die," he said. "Just don't lose it in the meantime! And mail this letter for me." He reached toward his table.

I felt like saying, "A bit bossy tonight, aren't we?" but I didn't. I knew the grumpiness was preoperation stress. Instead I took the envelope he indicated.

"Another letter for Adam Hurlbert," I said. "Are you a big contributor or something?"

"Right. I'm a big contributor." He gave that little snort that passed for a laugh.

79

"Okay, so it's not money. It's letters of endorsement. It's questions about his platform. It's—"

"None of your business," he cut in.

I made a face at him, but he was right. I backed off.

"Now promise me you'll come see me as soon as they let you, okay?" he said. "I told them you were like family and they should let you in whenever they decide I'm not going to kick the bucket."

"You're not going to die. You're too ornery."

He liked that and smiled at me.

I smiled warmly back, but my heart was chilled by the thought that he had written all those instructions for me. Me, for heaven's sake. How tragic to have lived sixty-five years and have no one closer than a friend of a few days' acquaintance.

SEVEN

Summer still filled the air when school began the Wednesday after Labor Day, but new notebooks, new teachers, and new outfits—to say nothing of a surfeit of summer boredom—made the transition easier for the kids. I was surprised at how glad I was to be back, though I despaired of ever learning the names of all my students. To cover my ignorance, I smiled a lot. My jaws ached each afternoon when I unglued my fingers and scrubbed the paint from under my nails.

Teaching elementary school art is fun. The kids don't yet feel it uncool to enjoy the class, and most of them are willing to try anything I ask. Much as I wished I could make a living from my painting, I enjoyed helping little fingers create something original, even if only a mother would call it lovely.

A few students, though, drove me to distraction—like Nelson Carmody Hurlbert. That boy was enough to make any adult vote against his stepfather in protest. If the man couldn't control a child, how would he ever manage the federal government?

But most of us at school excused the would-be senator because he and his lovely wife, Irene, had married when Nelson was eight, and the child's obnoxiousness was already well ingrained. Of course, if Adam won, he'd be getting involved with a national government that was over two hundred years old. Talk about ingrained bad habits.

Evenings I collapsed before my TV and watched Adam and

the ever-smiling Irene, sans Nelson, dash around the state making well-crafted speeches and shaking hands with everyone in sight. I hated to admit it, but Todd had been right about how much I'd enjoy the television.

The Key—it had taken on such a life that I thought of it with a capital letter—lay on my bureau day after day. Whenever I looked at it, I prayed for Mr. Geohagan. He was stabilizing nicely following his bypass surgery, and he'd soon be going home. My heart ached for him because he seemed utterly alone. I never saw anyone else visiting him, and he never mentioned anyone. I stopped in almost every day just to give him someone to talk to besides hospital staff.

But after he was well? Maybe he wouldn't need—or want—me then.

On the farm, harvesting was progressing at a fine rate. The eating corn was in, and the cattle corn was almost ready. It was the tomatoes that occupied everyone's efforts now. Ruth was completing a two-week leave from the pretzel factory to help harvest the fruit that lay rosy and fragrant in the fields. Even Mary left her kitchen to join her family for the gathering.

"We've got to finish today," John said at lunch on Saturday. A scowl hung on his normally expressionless face. "A big storm's coming, according to the weatherman." John had a battery-powered forecaster he kept in the barn and used daily for weather forecasts. "What we don't get in will be ruint, and we don't want that, eh?"

"Let me help," I said as I sliced a piece of Mary's homemade oatmeal bread. "I don't know much about farms, but I know how to pick tomatoes. My mom always grew several vines because she liked to can her own tomato juice."

I glanced up to see the family looking at me, and I wondered if they'd look any more surprised if I'd grown a second head.

"I mean it," I said. "I'll help."

I couldn't quite hide my smile at the picture we women made walking down the road to the tomato fields. Ruth and Mary were in their caped dresses while I wore my oldest jeans and a baggy T-shirt with a huge sunflower I'd silk-screened way back in some college art class. Their hair was neatly tucked beneath their kapps while mine, made flyaway by the humidity, was tucked behind my ears, from which dangled red, yellow, green, and blue triangles of various sizes. I wore sunglasses with mottled red frames while they both squinted. Ruth had her pink flip-flops on, Mary a much darned pair of black stockings and black shoes, and I had on a pair of scruffy sneakers with a hole by the left big toe.

"We used to grow tobacco on this acreage, like most of our neighbors," said Ruth as she fell in step beside me. Mary walked a bit behind but close enough to talk with us if she wanted to.

"When did you change?" I asked.

"About ten years ago. My older brother Andy kept telling Father that tobacco was a sinful crop—which didn't make Father too happy. Andy said that if we believed our bodies were the temple of the Holy Spirit like the Bible says, then we wouldn't be growing a crop that was harmful to the body. I don't think Father cared about being a temple and all because everyone raises tobacco, but he hoped that by going along with Andy he could keep him from *fremder Glawwe.*"

I shook my head; the phrase wasn't familiar.

"Strange belief," Ruth explained. "Andy was starting to go to church with Jon Clarke, and that got him asking all kinds of questions. Father was trying to stop him from turning away. I was only a little kid, but I remember the day Andy told Father he thought you could be certain of your salvation." There was shock in her voice even now.

"You don't agree?"

"Oh, no. You can't know for sure until you die. It's prideful to assume salvation, and sinful."

"Oh. I see." Then she'd undoubtedly think me prideful and a terrible sinner. I believed the Bible said you could be certain of your salvation. *My sheep listen to my voice,* Jesus said about those who believed in him. *I know them, and they follow me. I give them eternal life, and they shall never perish; no one can snatch them out of my hand.*

"You probably know our Andy," said Mary, who had moved up to walk with us. "He goes to your church."

"Andy Zook is your Andy?" I said in surprise. "I never made the connection, I guess because Zook is such a common name around here. He was my Sunday-school teacher last year. I think he and Sally are wonderful."

Mary nodded, but her smile was sad.

"He looks like John," I said, the light suddenly dawning. "I don't know how I could have missed it before. And Jake. He looks like a happy Jake."

I laughed, and Mary permitted herself a wry little chuckle.

"You'd never know it now, but he was such a happy little boy, Jake was," Mary said. "Always in trouble but happy. And Andy was such a good boy. He loved helping John in the barn."

I thought of Andy, tried to imagine him growing up here on the farm, wearing a Dutch-boy bob and a black felt hat. I thought of a little Jake running around in broadfall trousers and suspenders.

I wondered which son had hurt Mary more, the one with

the strong faith that disagreed with hers or the one with no faith.

Mary looked up and scanned the skies. "You'd never think it was going to rain, would you?"

I dutifully surveyed the brilliant blue heavens with their billowy cumulus clouds. "You surely wouldn't."

We walked in silence for a few minutes. I thought about the way Mary moved up beside Ruth and me when the conversation turned to issues of belief. Did Mary see me as a threat to Ruth, the one to lead another child from the community? Possibly. I didn't mean to cause any problem, but my sunflower and dangley earrings and ardent faith apart from the Ordnung might seem an attractive alternative to a young woman who felt hedged in—if Ruth felt hedged in, and I saw no signs that she did.

I again marveled at Mary and John. Trying to balance Jake's unique needs against keeping Ruth and Elam spiritually safe was quite a circus act. It required great skill in the art of compromise, and I was increasingly struck by the fine line these parents walked.

"See those flatbed wagons?" asked Ruth, unaware of any potentially significant byplay. She pointed with pride. "There's the one we filled yesterday."

The wagons stood at the field's edge, one with baskets stacked pyramid style on it. Mary, apparently satisfied with the innocuous topic, dropped behind us again.

"Tonight the truck will come from Campbell's Soup and pull them away. They come every day or two during picking season."

"I'm going to be picking Campbell's tomato soup?" I was fascinated by the idea. "The Campbells are coming, hoo-rah, hoo-rah."

I soon found out there was nothing to sing about in picking tomatoes. In a very short time my back ached unbearably, and my hands were green from the juice of the vine. The acrid smell of the plant was everywhere, and the sun was baking every drop of moisture from my body. Next thing I knew, I'd be hallucinating about a bottle of Evian water.

"If it gets to be too much, Kristie, you can stop anytime," said Mary when she offered me a drink of absolutely delicious water from the picnic thermos she'd brought. Never had water tasted so sweet and cool. "We appreciate all you've already done."

I stretched painfully, listening to my back creak as it never had before. My neck felt permanently elongated like a turtle's, my fingers were stiff , and my nails would give a manicurist a heart attack. I watched Ruth moving among the plants, her nimble fingers relentless in their search for fruit. At the field's edge Elam was lifting filled baskets to John who stood splay legged on a flatbed, the better to swing the load to its place in the pyramid.

Now I knew why the Amish went to chiropractors so often. I'd have to go along on the family's next visit. If I could wait that long.

I rubbed the small of my back and breathed deeply.

"Oh, I'm doing fine, Mary," I lied as I brushed my hair off my forehead. "I'll work as long as the rest of you. Todd's not coming till six-thirty, so I have plenty of time."

The afternoon was an endless haze of agony, of plant after plant and row after row. It was sweat dripping off the end of my nose and spiders lurking for me beneath leaves. I became resigned to the fact that I was going to walk bent over for the rest of my life and only be able to paint caterpillars and insects and dirt—the only things I'd ever be seeing. I knew I'd never have another bowl of tomato soup again.

I jumped as a hand touched my shoulder. I straightened slowly, each vertebra shrieking in protest, to face a smiling Ruth.

"Father says we can stop now. We've gotten most of the tomatoes, and we've run out of baskets."

I tried to smile back. "Great," I mumbled.

We turned to walk back to the house, and there stood Clarke at the side of the road. He looked fresh and energetic and clean in his worn jeans and yellow knit shirt. My slumping shoulders dipped farther. Was there no end of clever ways I could make a good impression on this man?

"You look a bit tired," he said as we reached him.

"Perceptive of you," I said tartly.

He grinned that marvelous grin and fell into step with Ruth and me as we walked toward the house.

"Staying for dinner, Jon Clarke?" asked Ruth. "Mom went back a while ago to make it."

He nodded. "She already asked me, just as I was hoping she would. In fact, she sent me down to collect you."

Suddenly I saw my plans for the evening as less than inspired.

There was a soft plop and an explosion at our feet. I looked in disbelief at the tomato pulp and juice all over my thoroughly dirty left sneaker, staining it an anemic red-brown. I looked up just in time to see another tomato sail past and splat against the fence post.

"Elam! You've lost your touch," yelled Ruth as she broke into a run. "I'll have to help you." She ran toward her brother and a pile of rotting tomatoes.

"That's right. You help him, Ruth," shouted Clarke as he grabbed my hand. "He's going to need all the help he can get."

He began running across the field, dragging me behind him.

"I should have known better than to visit today. That shows what a five-year absence will do. Come on, Kristie. Hurry up."

"What in the world's going on?" I demanded, pulling my hand free.

"Tomato fight. It's a Zook tradition. John always lets the kids have a bang-up battle at the end of each year's harvest as a reward for all their hard work."

Two tomatoes zinged past my head, one falling harmlessly to the ground, the other bouncing off Clarke's chest. As juice and pulp dribbled down his shirt, a delighted Elam yelled, "Bull's eye!"

"That does it!" Clarke yelled. "Battle stations, Kristie!" He grabbed two tomatoes and threw.

"You're crazy!" I watched in disbelief as Elam dodged Clarke's tomatoes and threw another of his own. It hit Clarke in the leg.

"For a pacifist, you're an awfully good shot," Clarke called as he shook his leg free of seeds.

"Two to nothing," yelled Ruth. Elam was too busy laughing to talk.

"Come on, Kristie. Don't be so inhibited." Clarke threw, missed Elam, but caught Ruth on the skirt. "Can you imagine the chaos when the others were still home and Jake was well? It was great!"

"How did you get involved?"

"When I lived with my aunt and uncle, Mr. Zook would hire me to help with the harvest—corn, too, but that was never as much fun."

"I guess not. Ears of corn tend to hurt when they hit."

"Here!" He put a split tomato in my hand, juice and pulp oozing. "Throw!"

I stared at it a minute. Then something went *pop* inside. I wheeled and threw. I missed my target. In fact the tomato seemed to disintegrate as it traveled, and nothing was left by the time it reached the enemy camp. Still I laughed aloud.

"Good girl," said Clarke approvingly.

"Over hill, over dale," I sang as I bent for more ammunition. A tomato hit me, exploding amidships. I straightened abruptly, startled.

Clarke sputtered with laughter. "Ruth did it."

We pursued each other across the fields in the general direction of the house. Crushed fruit lay all about, offering a bounteous supply of ammunition. Even Hawk rushed madly about, barking happily, while the red hen squawked in agitation.

The piercing sound of someone whistling through his fingers got our attention. It was Jake at the edge of the road.

"Mom says dinner's in fifteen minutes." He studied us and shook his head. "You might want to clean up."

I looked at myself, then at the other three, and began to laugh.

"Even my hair," I said as I tried to run my fingers through the sticky mess. "Good grief, I'm too old for this."

"You're too old?" said Clarke. "I bet I've got a few years on you, and I haven't had such fun in ages."

We walked slowly down the road past the farm pond with Elam pushing Jake and Hawk loping beside us. The dog gave a sudden bark and detoured to the pond, ducking under the battery-charged electric fence that separated it and the adjoining pasture from the road. "He wants us to wait while he gets a drink," interpreted Ruth.

Hawk began drinking, his tail waving happily. It was a terrible surprise to him when the tail connected with the electric fence. The shock jolted him, and he let out a yelp as he jumped, landing ignominiously in the middle of the pond. While we dissolved in laughter, Hawk swam with great dignity to the shore, shook himself off, and stalked away, his feelings hurt.

"A car," gasped Elam as he tried to get his breath. "Behind us."

We crowded together on the shoulder to make room for the car. I looked up curiously and found myself staring into Todd's incredulous face.

EIGHT

I backed through Mr. Geohagan's door, staring down the hall in wonder at the retreating figure, tall and elegant with his prematurely white hair. An entourage of aides and a bevy of newsmen scurried about him, eager to do his bidding and report on his every word.

"Mr. Geohagan, did you see him?" I sank into the chair beside the bed, breathless as a schoolgirl who's seen a rock star. "That was Adam Hurlbert! He looks even better now than he did when he came to school that one time for Nelson. He wasn't a candidate then, and his hair wasn't quite so wonderfully white. Do you think he puts something on it? I bet he does!"

I knew I sounded like an idiot, but *Adam Hurlbert!* "I wonder what he's doing here at the hospital?"

Everett Geohagan, pale and frail, grinned lopsidedly and tried to look modest. "Visiting me."

"Visiting you? Then you are a big contributor!"

He shook his head and gave that little wheeze that was his laugh. "No, that's not it. I used to work for him."

"You did? You mean I know somebody who knows Somebody? That's almost as good as knowing Somebody myself."

When he laughed gently at me, I blushed. How naive and straight-off-the-farm I sounded. "Still," I defended myself, "it must be fun watching someone you know become famous."

Mr. Geohagan shrugged. "Are you going to vote for him?"

"I certainly am. Aren't you?"

"I suspect that all I'll be doing on Election Day is reading about the outcome here or in some blasted nursing home. But tell me. Why are you going to vote for Adam?"

I thought for a minute. "Well, he's very assured, very controlled. He makes you think he knows exactly what needs to be done and, by George, he's the one to do it. He's been well conceived and well packaged. If he's a fraction as knowledgeable about politics as he is about public relations, he'll be terrific. And he's a political novice. No back-room debts to pay."

"And perhaps no political savvy either?"

"You think not? You think it's all a well-rehearsed act? He doesn't really know anything?"

"Who knows?" said Mr. Geohagan. "I do know he's been successful at every other project he's put his mind to. He was a young vet just back from Vietnam when I first met him in the midseventies. The same week he got discharged, he formed Hurlbert Construction, and in the fall he started college at Franklin and Marshall full time. He finished college in three years and kept the company going the whole time. I was one of his first employees."

Mr. Geohagan shook his head at the memory. "One thing I'll say for Adam. He's never lacked ambition or self-confidence. In fact there are those who accuse him of overweening pride. I think he just decides what he wants, goes after it, and lets nothing stop him. 'We're going to be the biggest construction company Lancaster County has ever seen,' he said." Mr. Geohagan shrugged. "We are."

"Why do you think he decided to go into politics if he was so successful in business?"

"Power would be my guess. That and new worlds to conquer. People like him can get bored with things the rest of us would be more than content with. Of course, marrying the governor's widowed daughter was no drawback either."

Irene Parsons Carmody Hurlbert was fifteen years younger than her new husband, and their whirlwind courtship had been splashed all over the media. They even made the cover of *People*, and I followed every detail as avidly as everyone else— the meeting at a local party fund-raiser, the immediate spark, the glamorous courtship with dinners in Washington, D. C., and vacations in the Caribbean, the soft-soaping of Adam's nasty divorce of five years earlier, the huge wedding with the first lady and the vice president and his wife among the multitude of glamorous and politically well-connected guests. The bid for office was probably inevitable. So, I thought, was the outcome of his race against a sturdy but thoroughly uncharismatic opponent.

"Irene seems so gracious and charming, to say nothing of beautiful. Is she as wonderful as she appears?"

Mr. Geohagan smiled his sardonic, lopsided grin at me. "Did I ever tell you that you remind me of my daughter, Cathleen?"

"Why, thank you," I said in surprise. "What a lovely thing to say. But I didn't even know you had a daughter."

"I miss her terribly," he said. "I think that's why I enjoy you so much."

"Do I look like her?"

"Not particularly. I've always thought of her as absolutely beautiful."

I swallowed hard. Not that people tell me I'm beautiful on a regular basis, but this was the most direct repudiation I'd ever had, even if unintentional. Mr. Geohagan didn't seem to notice.

"She had red-gold hair that was naturally curly," he said. "Not straight brown hair like you. And she had great dark eyes.

Of course, you have marvelous dark eyes too," he hastened to add. Maybe he'd seen something in my face, or maybe he was just as politically astute as Adam Hurlbert. "You're very pretty in your own way. But you don't look like her. You've got a square jaw, and you're too skinny. She had a wonderful figure, full in all the right places."

I put on my polite face, trying not to become too depressed by his assessment of my assets. After all, a man's daughter should be beautiful to him.

He studied me a minute. "You've got pale, creamy skin. She had the cutest freckles across her nose, and they drove her crazy. I thought they were adorable."

"Does she live far away?" I hoped this paragon lived in Washington or Oregon or maybe up at Hudson's Bay so that I'd never have to compete.

"She's dead." The statement was bald and unemotional.

"Oh." It was more an involuntary rush of air than a word. I felt like I'd been kicked by an Amishman's mule.

"Don't look so upset," he said. "It's not your fault."

"No, but—" I was at a loss for words.

"In case you haven't noticed, life's not always nice," he said with more than a touch of bitterness.

We sat silently, thinking about life's low blows.

"But," he said after a minute, "you bring me great pleasure with your interest in me and my health. I love your enthusiasm for life. Cathleen was that way, always bubbling, always happy. She lived for fun and parties and going out. She always said that people were the most interesting things on the face of the earth, and she had loads of friends. Everyone loved her because she loved them, and she could talk to anybody about anything. She was our sunshine."

She didn't sound much like introverted, intense me, but if it made him happy to think of her when he looked at me, that was fine.

"If I'd listened to her," he said, "I wouldn't be in such a bad fix now. 'Stop smoking, Dad,' she'd always say. 'It's bad for you. You'll get cancer.' I'd laugh at her earnest young face and keep right on. Three packs a day. Then one day I couldn't go up the steps without puffing, but it wasn't cancer. Emphysema. 'Oh, Dad,' she said. 'I'm so sorry.'"

He gazed sadly out his window. "She didn't know it, but she didn't know what sorry meant then. Not then. And neither did I, though I sure do now. Now I have to blow into those foolish machines for the nurses. Or try to blow up balloons. Or listen to lectures by respiratory therapists about the evils of smoking."

I looked at him with concern. "I didn't know you had emphysema."

"There's a lot about me you don't know, young lady." His voice had a bit more life to it. "I've had it for about five years now. Or it's had me. I've got about five years left to live, they say—if something else doesn't get me first. I have a heart condition, a lung condition, and a blood condition."

I knew about the heart and now the lungs, but a blood condition?

"I'm a full-service patient." Sardonic anger tinged his voice. "It doesn't matter what your medical specialty, I'm your man."

"What blood condition?"

"I've got hepatitis. Maybe I got it from the transfusions I got during my surgery, maybe not. Who knows? But I've got it, and that's what counts. Didn't you see the sign on the door? I'm contagious."

I got up and walked to the door. I pulled it open and there was the very obvious sign warning me not to touch anything and to wash thoroughly if I did. I must have been too taken with Adam Hurlbert to notice it.

"You're looking at a human pin cushion," Mr. Geohagan grumped. "Did you know there's one nurse whose only job is to go around all day taking blood from people? That's all she does—stab people! What a job, sucking the lifeblood from already ill people. She only gets away with it because we're too weak and sick to fight her off."

I came back to my seat. "Now, you know you're lucky to have someone like her caring for you. You should be thanking God instead of griping."

"See? That's just the kind of in-your-face, cheer-me-up comment Cathleen would have made. I told you you were like her." He nodded approval. "And I need cheering up. Did you know they're going to send me to some blasted nursing home as soon as the hepatitis clears up? With sick, old people! And they'll probably try and make me stay there forever."

I shook my head. "You can't stay there forever. You told me yourself that you've got too much to do."

"I do," he agreed. "I've got lots to do, and it needs to be done now! And I can't do it stuck in here!"

My heart went out to him. "What can I do to help? Just tell me."

"See? Cathleen. There are a couple of things you can do, actually. I was just hoping you'd ask." He handed me a piece of paper and a key.

I looked at the key. "Another one? Do I have to keep *it* for life too?"

"Don't get all worked up. It belongs to my apartment. Would you go over and get some books and things for me? I've written down everything I want, and I've drawn you a map."

I read the list written in a spidery hand and looked at the

96

map with its tremulous streets.

"Why, you live near my school," I said. "I have to go to Parents' Night tonight. I'll stop for your things on the way and bring them to you tomorrow. Is that soon enough?"

His appreciative smile made the slight inconvenience negligible.

"The apartment isn't much," he said. "Cathleen never lived there. We had a wonderful house in the country, but…" His voice trailed off.

All the way home I thought about Everett Geohagan. Here was a man who hurt both physically and emotionally. His weakened body might or might not recover from its multiple attacks. And he deeply mourned for Cathleen, obviously much loved. How long had it been since her death? How old was she when she died? What did she die from?

And where was Mrs. Geohagan? For there to be a Cathleen, there had to be such a lady. Was she dead too? Was that why I was the errand runner, the keeper of The Key? Or were they divorced and she was no longer involved in his life?

Full of unanswered questions and frustration because I couldn't fix any of Mr. Geohagan's real problems, I arrived home just in time to be included in dinner. We gathered around the oilcloth-covered table and bowed our heads for the silent grace. Mary's chicken and stuffing went around the table, as did the fresh beets, beans, and tomatoes.

"Guess who I saw today?" I asked as I spread some apple butter on Mary's delicious potato rusk.

The five Zooks asked "Who?" with their eyebrows.

"Adam Hurlbert!"

Ruth looked at me blankly. "Who?"

"Adam Hurlbert. You know. The man who's running for senator."

"I'm afraid I don't know him either," said Elam.

The cultural gap yawned wide at my feet. I'd forgotten that politics were a foible of the fancy.

"I've seen him on TV," said Jake. "Tall, handsome, white hair, too many teeth. Beautiful wife. Hurlbert Construction."

"That's him," I said.

"Hurlbert Construction? I know the company name," said Elam. "I've seen their equipment and projects around."

"They're the ones that built the motel and restaurant on what used to be Fishers' farm, ain't?" asked John. "They put all that rich, black soil under macadam?"

Elam nodded. "That's them."

John looked up from his chicken. "And you seen him today?"

"At the hospital. He was visiting Mr. Geohagan because Mr. Geohagan used to work for him."

"Well, if you see him again, tell him to leave the farmland alone." John returned to his chicken.

"Okay," I said, though I couldn't imagine doing any such thing. "But he's Mr. Geohagan's friend, not mine."

"And how is your friend coming along?" Mary asked.

"I think he's doing all right, but he has emphysema and hepatitis, and they're complicating his recovery. He's going to have to go to a nursing home, and that scares and angers him."

I washed down a mouthful of bread stuffing with sweetened iced tea. "Today he told me I reminded him of his daughter Cathleen, though I'm not as pretty."

"He actually said that?" asked Ruth, aghast. "But you're beautiful."

"Ruth," said Mary in quiet reprimand. Compliments led to pride.

I blushed. "Thanks, Ruth." I wondered again what she really thought of me and my makeup and brightly colored clothing and yellow car.

One evening last week she and I had washed the dinner dishes together. She was talking about the new dress she was sewing.

"Would you ever wear a pink or yellow dress?" I asked. I knew red, my favorite color, was out of the question. It was the color for harlots. But the soft colors? "God made those hues too. Just look at the flowers."

"Oh, I'd never wear bold things like that," Ruth said, immediately rejecting the idea. "I wouldn't want to wear anything that called attention to myself."

I nodded, thinking that if I dressed the way she did, I'd be doing exactly what she wanted to avoid. It all came down to who you hung around with.

"Cathleen," said Jake from his place across the table from me. "Cathleen Geohagan. Why does that name sound familiar?"

We all looked at him expectantly, but he shook his head. "It'll come. Just give me a few minutes."

I was finishing my last spoonful of cornstarch pudding when Jake yelled, "Aha! I have it."

"Tell me," I said.

"I read about her in the Lancaster paper six or seven months ago. I remember because she used to date one of the guys I worked with at the trailer plant before she threw him over for some other guy. Broke my friend's heart, but that's another story."

"That was in the paper?"

"Very funny," said Jake as he took more pudding. "Actually I read about her death. She killed herself with pills and booze."

NINE

I was stunned. I saw Mr. Geohagan lying in his bed, hands resting on his stomach, eyes staring at memories.

"I miss her," he had said. I'll just bet he did.

"I remember something else about her death," Jake said. "It was her parents who found her, and it was too much for the mother."

"She died too?" I was afraid of the answer.

Jake shook his head. "I don't think so. She just had a stroke or something like that."

Just a stroke, I thought. Just a stroke. No wonder she never came to visit! As we bowed our heads for the silent postdinner prayer, all I could think about was poor Mr. Geohagan.

Oh, Lord, he needs you so badly! How can I help him find you?

I left early for Parents' Night so I'd have time to detour to Mr. Geohagan's apartment. I wore the conservative navy skirt that I'd worn when I came to meet the Zooks for the first time. I even wore the white blouse. Anything to impress the parents with how trustworthy I was. But I probably shot the whole conservative image with my silver-studded denim blazer, the product of another art class. I particularly like the great appliquéd pumpkin on the back and the artfully arranged fall foliage at its base.

I followed Mr. Geohagan's directions in a blue funk. I'm good at feeling depressed even when nothing's wrong. "You may have a sensitive artist's nature," my mother used to say when I got overly melancholy, "but that's no excuse to inflict your pessimism on the rest of us. Rain on your own parade if you must, but not on mine. Now shape up or spend the day in your room."

I've learned to spare the general populace my blue periods as I've matured, but tonight I felt justified in being positively morose. Even my sunshine car couldn't relieve my dark mood.

As I walked down the long, dingy hall of an unimpressive tan brick apartment building, I studied the door numbers, looking for number 10. I was nonplused when I found two 9s, until I realized that the first was a 6 whose top screw had come out, causing the number to rotate 180 degrees—a great metaphor for the condition of the building. Everything was a dirty, dreary beige. Even the straw wreath someone had hung on number 5 was shaggy and uninspiring. The brass plate on number 8 was so tarnished and pitted that it looked like wrought iron.

I found the door I was looking for at the end of the hall and turned the key silently in the lock. I felt like a cat burglar, sneaking about where I had no business. I imagined a neighbor calling the police, and I couldn't help wondering whether my principal would see the humor if I were arrested. I glanced furtively down the hall, then quickly opened and closed the door.

It was no surprise to find the apartment as depressing as the hallway. No smiling family pictures in gilt frames personalized the rooms. Nothing hung on the walls or sat on the end tables to lighten a grayness made of equal parts approaching night and gloomy atmosphere. It was more than obvious that Cathleen and Mrs. Geohagan had never lived here. No woman could have stood the sterility.

I walked to the single bedroom and stood in the doorway staring. The double bed was unmade, left just as it had been that day when Mr. Geohagan became ill. A pair of gray trousers hung from the closet doorknob, the legs pooling into wrinkles. A plastic hamper held a pair of dirty blue socks and some underwear, and the dresser top was empty except for a sprinkling of small change.

I put the pants on a hanger after hand pressing them flat and stuck them in the closet. I quickly made the bed. I couldn't help wondering if the pants would ever be worn or the bed slept in again. I smoothed the bedspread carefully over the single pillow. A double bed should never have just one pillow!

Feeling even more deeply melancholy, I gathered the stationery and paperback westerns I had come for, found the pajamas and underwear, the slippers and robe. I slipped them into the canvas tote bag I'd brought; then I stood by the window and looked out at the gathering night, resting my head against the pane. I felt tears very near the surface.

Suddenly, with all the sound and fury of crashing surf, the toilet in the bathroom flushed.

I froze, shocked into paralysis.

Water rushed from the bathroom tap as someone—someone who shouldn't be here!—washed his hands.

Are clean thieves nicer than dirty ones? *Help, Lord!*

I heard the bathroom door open, and I grabbed my chest to keep my heart from popping right through my ribcage. Where to hide?

For want of a better place I rushed to the closet, pocketbook and tote bag thumping against the wall as I ran. I pulled the door quietly closed after me, hoping the muffled thuds hadn't been audible to anyone but me. I held my breath and pressed my ear to the door.

I heard footfalls as he came into the bedroom. And stopped. I could almost feel his surprise right through the door.

The bed! I had made the bed! If he had been in this room before, he now knew someone else was in the apartment. And I had told him.

He walked from the bedroom, and I strained to hear. Maybe he'd missed the significance of the bed and was just going to leave. There obviously wasn't anything in this place worth taking.

Then again, maybe he wasn't leaving. Over the thudding alarms of my heart I could hear him moving from room to room, undoubtedly looking for the newly arrived maid. I was doomed.

I pulled the light cord hanging over my head and looked wildly for some clever place to hide. Hanging from the rod were a half dozen shirts and three pairs of slacks including the ones I had just put there. No hope of concealment there. But the top shelf was completely empty. I could hide there.

Yeah, right. Even if I'd been able to scramble up there on thin air, I'd be a bit obvious when the door was wrenched open.

Once, years ago, I'd seen a cowboy movie on TV in which the hero and his girl hid from the bad guys in a closet. He stashed her on a high shelf, and he lay on the floor. When the villains shot through the door, the good guys were safe.

Such a ploy was extremely clever if you knew the bad guys would only shoot at the middle of the door. I stared at the floor, weighing whether being safe from bullets (aimed only at the middle of the door) was worth the risk of being found curled in an extremely vulnerable position if the door were wrenched abruptly open.

Suddenly from the other side of the door, the door I was actually leaning on, came the most malevolent chuckle I had ever heard. I leaped away from the wood as if it were aflame.

Lord, help!

There were sliding noises and a grunt or two, and I realized my villain had made his move. He wasn't going to shoot me; he wasn't even going to open the door. There was no need. He was just going to block me in.

I reached for the doorknob and pushed wildly. The only response was another wicked chuckle from the other side, followed by some more sliding. Then silence.

I drew back into a far corner, feeling defenseless and frightened. Every crime and gothic flick I'd ever seen flooded my mind. The images did nothing for my nerves, especially since I knew I had no knight in shining armor to rush to my rescue.

I crouched in my corner and shivered and prayed and listened. I was unpleasantly aware of the watcher standing on his side of the door, waiting just as I was.

Lord, help!

Suddenly there was movement in the room. I crept to the door and listened. Whoever was out there must have grown tired of waiting and had begun searching the place. I could hear drawers being pulled open, sometimes falling to the floor as if wrenched off their tracks.

What was the person searching for? Certainly anyone could see that there was nothing of value in this lonely, godforsaken place.

Lord, help!

Gradually my heart slowed, and my pulse rate returned to near normal. It appeared the thief had no interest in me. In fact, he seemed to have forgotten me. He was now in the living room, now the kitchen, taking no care to be quiet with his movements. He knew that the location of the apartment, first-floor corner, largely did away with being heard by neighbors. Besides, he was probably hurrying as fast as he could. I might have friends.

I got down on my knees and tried to peer under the door. All I could see was more of the rug that covered the closet floor, a very unattractive shade of brown, perfect for a drab place like this.

I slumped in my corner and waited, willing the intruder to leave. Finally I heard the front door slam. I jumped to my feet and listened. All remained quiet.

Thank you, Lord!

I twisted the doorknob and pushed wildly, hoping against hope that whatever was blocking me in would move. It didn't. That would have been too easy.

I turned and leaned my back against the door, pushing, pushing while the slick soles of my new shoes sought traction on the carpeting. Suddenly my feet flew out from under me, and I grabbed at the nearest thing, an old red-and-blue plaid shirt, to keep from falling. I fell anyway, my spine bouncing hard in spite of the rug. The shirt landed on my head, its collar button popped by the pull of my weight. The malformed hanger bounced noiselessly beside me.

I got to my feet, rubbing my sore back. This time I faced the door, placed my palms flat, straightened my arms, and shoved as hard as I could. Nothing happened except my shoulders, still tender from the tomato picking and fighting, protested what they obviously felt was more abuse.

I stared at the door, trying to picture what was piled against it out there in the free world. The dresser? The bed? Both?

The hinges! The idea burst like an epiphany, and I was thoroughly impressed with my cleverness. I would take the hinges apart the way my father did whenever he painted a door, sliding out the little round things that slid down into those little circles. Then I'd pull the door loose and climb out.

But the thoughtless builder had put the hinges on the room side of the door, not on my side.

All right. I'd just power the door down.

I rammed it with my shoulder a couple of times, astonished at how abruptly I bounced back. Rubbing my soon-to-be-black-and-blue shoulder, I quickly and decisively rejected physical force.

I think I realized then that I wasn't going to escape. I don't know how else to explain my screaming, pounding fit. When my fists were too sore to continue, I stopped my ridiculous behavior. Maybe later on tonight when I might be more easily heard, I could try again, this time in conscious choice.

I sat cross-legged with my back against the wall. I looked at the Louis L'Amour and Max Brand books that had tumbled from the tote bag. I needed to introduce Mr. Geohagan to Steve Bly and Sigmund Brouwer. Get him reading some Christian westerns.

I picked up one of the paperbacks. I might as well pass the time profitably. If I thought of Mr. Edgars, my principal, storming up and down the halls looking for me, I'd only upset myself more. I glanced at my watch. I was already a half hour late.

Please, God! Let Mr. Edgars sound the alarm.

I glanced at the weak bulb on the ceiling and wondered how damaged my eyes would become reading in this dimness.

The light! No wonder the intruder had known exactly where I was. The glow must have shown around the edges of the door in the almost dark room. Sighing at my stupidity, I began reading.

I understood that I was in the closet for the night when my

second and third screaming and pounding fits brought no more response than my first—unless you counted a sore throat and tender, tender hands. My watch said 1:00 A.M.

I began to feel sorry for myself big time. Here I was, missing for the night, and no one cared enough to come and get me. Apparently no one even missed me. I felt the tears rise.

I blinked them back. After all, I was a strong, modern, independent woman. So what that I was trapped, thirsty, hungry, and in need of a bathroom. So what that if I wanted to sleep, I would have to do so on the floor. Who cared that it was getting chillier all the time and that I had no covers and that I couldn't even stretch out all the way because the closet was too small. The pioneers had survived worse situations that this, and so would I. I was tough. I could take it.

Sighing, I turned out the light and lay on my back with a couple of Mr. Geohagan's shirts and his bathrobe over me for warmth and my knees bent so I would fit. I stuck a couple of the paperbacks under my head for a pillow. Every time I moved, I slipped off, thonking my skull on the floor.

"I want Clarke to come and rescue me," I said aloud into the darkness. Then I giggled. "Now where did that come from?"

But I couldn't deny the idea had a certain appeal. He could blast me free with an Uzi, something all Christian counselors keep hidden under their mattresses. Or he could push the offending furniture away and throw the door open while I huddled beguilingly on the top shelf, just waiting to be grasped by the waist and lowered tenderly to the floor. Or he could loosen the hinges—they were on his side—and manhandle the door open, lifting me from my swoon (from lack of food and water, not fear) and carrying me to safety in his strong arms. Who cared that if he got to the hinges, he wouldn't need to do anything but pull the door open. Rescues demanded marvelous feats performed on behalf of the damsel in distress.

Obviously being in the dark in small, closed places wasn't good for me.

Lord, I have the distinct feeling that this is one of those situations in which I have to choose. You saved me from potential physical harm earlier this evening, and I thank you most sincerely. But somehow this is the harder part, isn't it? Somehow sleeping in this dumb closet on this hard floor is going to develop me as a Christian—if I choose to let it. I can keep pitying myself, or I can just trust you.

I sighed. *I'll trust.*

I actually slept, my slumber interspersed with abrupt awakenings every time my head slid off the books.

In the morning, I had read the fourth Louis L'Amour book and prayed most thoroughly for everyone I had ever known when, at about nine o'clock, I heard someone at the front door.

"In here!" I yelled. "I'm in here!"

"Don't worry! I'm coming," yelled a male voice. I had no idea whom it belonged to. I just knew it wasn't my hero.

There was much scraping and grunting, but finally the door of my prison opened, and a gray-haired policeman stood there, a middle-aged angel in blue. He was somewhat startled when I threw my arms around his neck and hugged him hard. Then I almost knocked him over in my rush for the bathroom.

"I'm all right. Truly I am," I said to Mr. Geohagan. "No scars, bumps, or bruises." My sore fists didn't count.

"But you might have been badly hurt!"

I patted his thin hand as it lay on the covers. "But I wasn't. I'm just sorry it was necessary for you to be informed."

"No one knew where I lived. They had to contact me so

they'd know where to find you. I just can't believe it took them until today!"

I made a wry face. "Me neither, but I understand how it happened. Last night Mary and Ruth assumed they'd just missed seeing me. John wouldn't have noticed whether I was there or not, and Jake would have been in his own apartment all evening. I think Mr. Edgars was pretty angry with me when I didn't show for Parents' Night, but he assumed that for some reason of my own I had decided not to come. He planned to get me about it this morning when I came to work.

"This morning Mary was very concerned when I didn't come down to breakfast. She finally checked my bed, and—surprise, surprise—it hadn't been slept in. Jake finally called my school at Mary's insistence, and it became obvious as he talked with Mr. Edgars that I hadn't been seen after I left the house last evening. Jake remembered I was coming to your place, and he called the police."

"And they called me. Let me tell you, I thought I was going to have another coronary. The news that you were okay was such a relief!"

I was touched by his concern.

"And you didn't see the thief?" he asked.

"Not a glimpse. The laughter I heard through the closet door was so deep that I'm certain it was a man, but that's all I know. I'm just sorry your apartment was ransacked. The man did a thorough job of it."

Mr. Geohagan shook his head. "I don't care about the apartment. It was only somewhere to sleep. It wasn't my house. I sold that shortly after Cathleen died and Doris became sick. I just couldn't stand being there anymore. There's nothing in that apartment I'd miss—except you."

"That's so sweet," I said, smiling, but I was struck again by the emptiness of his life.

Lord, I'm alone too. Don't let me ever have a life that barren. Please! And help me fill some of the holes in his life.

I handed him today's *Intelligencer Journal*.

"You were right," I said, pointing to page one. "Sick calls are indeed good copy. Now you're famous."

He looked at the front-page picture of himself and Adam Hurlbert shaking hands. Hurlbert had health and vitality oozing from every pore. Even his toothy smile had vigor. Mr. Geohagan looked worse than ever by contrast. The black-and-white picture drained what little color he had and left him looking cadaverous.

"How convenient for Adam that I chose this time to become ill," he said cynically.

"But not very convenient for you. You need to get better so you can get back to normal living. You've got all that stuff to do!"

"Nothing's normal about my life anymore," he said, his bitterness and self-pity kicking in with a vengeance. "My daughter's dead, my wife's had a stroke and doesn't even know me, and I'm sick, sick, sick!"

Forcing down my sympathy, I said, "To what do we owe your rousing good spirits? I'm the one who spent the night in the closet, not you."

To my surprise, Mr. Geohagan laughed. "Just like Cathleen. That slight touch of hauteur when upset. You're so good for me, Kristie."

I smiled. "I'm glad."

"You'd have liked her," Mr. Geohagan said. "She was a marvelous girl until—" He stopped abruptly.

"Until?" I prompted automatically, then regretted speaking

for fear I'd overstepped my bounds. Though I reminded him of his daughter, I didn't have the right to pry into family business. When he finally began to speak, I was relieved.

"Until she met this man. Isn't it always a man?"

I nodded obligingly.

"She moved out of our house and into an apartment of her own. Then he dumped her, and she couldn't handle it. She began drinking and taking massive doses of relaxants that she got for a 'sore back.' One night she took too much of both." Mr. Geohagan sighed with utter desolation. "And I don't know if it was an accident or not."

My heart lurched. To not know whether your daughter committed suicide must be the only thing worse than knowing she did.

"Her mother and I found her lying on the floor in the bathroom. Doris had become concerned because we hadn't heard from her for a few days and couldn't get her on the phone."

Mr. Geohagan stared out the window. "She was a fairy child. Quick, happy, beautiful, born long after we despaired of ever having a baby. Even her teen years were joyous. She never had the traumas that others had. Everyone loved her, and she them—until the affair collapsed."

Mr. Geohagan folded and refolded his sheet, making linen accordion pleats. "Not that we minded the relationship—at least not at first," he hastened to assure me. "The man was a fine man."

"You really didn't mind?"

Mr. Geohagan looked surprised. "Of course not. It's not like she was sixteen. She was twenty-one, a woman. A wonderful woman. And I'll never forgive God for letting her die."

I started, not because what he said shocked me but because he spoke the last sentence with such animosity.

Mr. Geohagan saw my expression. "My feelings toward God shock you, don't they?"

"Sadden me," I said, but he didn't hear.

"I have no time for him." The hard edge in his voice could have cut steel. "Where was he when Cathleen was hurting? When Doris had her stroke? No." He shook his head. "I have no time for a 'loving God' who would allow that to happen."

He closed his eyes, his bitterness wrapped around him like a cloak. "Why don't you come and see me the day after tomorrow?"

TEN

As the days passed, I found myself much preoccupied with concern for Mr. Geohagan and uncertainty about Todd.

I knew there was little I could do for Mr. Geohagan except pray for him and visit him whenever I could manage it. A few minutes of my time was a small price to pay for the smile he gave me when I entered his room and the gentle teasing I suffered at his hand.

"Why aren't you married?" he asked me one day. "You must have a secret flaw I haven't found yet."

Or, "Didn't you ever hear of good taste? That purple-and-pink thing you're wearing has a crooked front, and the colors boggle the mind."

"It's not purple and pink," I protested. "It's mauve, lavender, and lilac. And it's not a thing; it's a sweater. And it's not crooked; it's called an asymmetrical opening. And I'll have you know I made it."

"I knew that." And he grinned.

"You," I said, "are a mean old man."

I began to pray more and more that by my love and concern I would show him the heart of the God he was so angry at. I wanted his bitterness to be lost in the embrace of God's love.

~ ~ ~ ~ ~

Todd was another story.

"If only he were a jerk," I told Hawk one Friday evening as we sat together on the front steps. Since the night in the closet, I hadn't allowed myself to daydream about Clarke, but the fact that I had done so once threw my feelings for Todd into a starker light than ever before. "But he can be so nice, and I don't want to hurt him."

Hawk looked at me with his tongue lolling off to one side. His eyes held sympathy for my dilemma, though what he'd say if he knew Todd had once called him mangy, I could only imagine.

"Do you often talk to dogs?"

I started and looked at Jake as he wheeled up beside me. "Geez, guy! Do you always sneak up on people? That's twice you've gotten me."

He grinned, unrepentant. "There might as well be something good about this chair. If sneaking is it, then I'll take it."

I shook my head in mock indignation. "You're a mess. And yes, I like talking to dogs. They never sass or complain, and they always look so interested and intelligent. And they run right up to you, announcing themselves with barks and wiggles, not like some sneaky people I know. What more could I ask of a companion?"

Jake reached out to Hawk, and the dog immediately deserted me.

"Of course, faithfulness and loyalty might be nice," I said.

Jake laughed and ran his hand gently over the dog's head. "Tell me, Hawk, what should I do with my life? What should Kristie do with hers?"

Hawk wagged his tail happily.

"Should I stay forever on this farm?" he asked. "Should she

115

marry that Todd person? Give us your answers, please."

Hawk placed his forepaws on Jake's knees, raised himself, and licked Jake's face in great, moist swipes.

"What are you going to do with your life?" I asked as Hawk sank to the ground beside the wheelchair. "You must get bored sitting in your rooms all the time. I know I would."

"Bored? I don't know about that. My life may not seem very exciting to you, but it's safe and I like that. Look where risk and excitement got me." He slapped the side of his chair. "Some days sitting around is all I feel like doing."

"And it's enough just to be safe?"

"For now anyway."

"But it's so passive."

"In other words, I should get a life?"

I nodded, smiling to soften my words. "I had hoped I was a bit more tactful than that, but yeah. That's what I mean. What did you do before the accident? I think I heard you say you worked in a plant?"

"Yeah. I worked in a trailer fabricating plant riveting the shells of travel trailers together. There's no way I can do that now. You have to be completely mobile." He shrugged. "I don't have any other skills. After all, I left school at fourteen."

"Fourteen! I thought state law mandated sixteen as the youngest you can leave."

"Most Amish kids don't go beyond eighth grade. They're supposed to go to Saturday morning classes for another year to study religion, but no one cares much if it doesn't happen. Of course, Mom and Father always made us go. They always do everything the right way. I worked for Father here on the farm until I was eighteen. Then I went to the plant. Better money."

"Have you ever thought about getting a high school equivalency degree? It would allow you to find a better job or maybe even go to college."

"That's what Todd suggested."

I blinked. "Todd?"

"The last time he came out here, he brought me a book and some tapes from the Lancaster library. They're all about GEDs and how to get one. I spent a couple of hours this morning reading and listening." He shrugged again. "It was interesting enough, and I do like learning stuff. Maybe I'll try it someday."

"Oh, I think you should," I said too enthusiastically.

Jake raised an eyebrow, and I felt foolish. I sounded like I was encouraging one of my less academically nimble school kids.

"Well, you should," I said more quietly.

"Maybe someday," he repeated. "I've got a new toy to keep me occupied for a while now." He pointed to the dark green Caravan in the drive. "I finally took my driver's test for hand-controlled driving. Andy and Zeke have been after me to do it for some time. Even Father encouraged me as a way of getting me involved in life again. Then Jon Clarke started on me, too, and I finally got tired of fighting everyone. The same thing'll probably happen with the GED."

I stared at the van and wondered if Jake had always been so passive. Did he always need people pushing him, encouraging him, urging him on? Or was it a side effect of being disabled? Either way I was willing to be part of his cheering section if it would help him move forward.

But who was I to criticize? In my own way, I was just as passive, just as indecisive. I sighed.

"What's wrong?" Jake asked.

"Todd."

"What about him? He's losing interest? You're losing interest?"

"I don't know."

"He's an okay guy, Kristie." Jake grinned. "Maybe a bit stuffy and more than a little opinionated, but nice. The only thing is"—and Jake became very serious—"maybe nice isn't enough to marry on."

All night that thought flowed through my mind. *"Maybe nice isn't enough to marry on."* When I pulled myself from bed at six-thirty after a ragged night's sleep, it was the first thing I thought of. Maybe nice isn't enough to marry on.

I grabbed my robe and padded downstairs to the bathroom. As I walked through the kitchen, Mary and Ruth, already up for well over an hour, were finishing the breakfast cleanup. They were so cheerful I shuddered.

Maybe nice isn't enough to marry on.

I turned on the shower and let the hot water beat me awake. I put Todd from my mind and thought again about the wonderful ingenuity and expediency of the Amish. A motor in the house to pump the water for the shower would be anti-Ordnung, so a water tank on high stilts stood outside the shed. The water was pumped to the tank by a water wheel on the farm stream. From the tank it fell by gravity to the coal-fired water heater, was pumped by a battery-operated pump to the shower, and was therefore legal.

I toweled myself dry quickly and hurried upstairs to dress. The morning was brisk, forecasting colder days coming. Soon I'd be seeing my breath and longing for the comforts of central heating. I needed to look into a ceramic heater.

The big kitchen stove was still warm when I finally came

down, so I scrambled myself an egg and enjoyed it with a cup of tea and some potato rusk Mary had baked yesterday.

By seven-thirty Mary and I were in my car, ready to leave for the Bird-in-Hand Farmers' Market out on 340. The back of the car was filled with jars of Mary's delicious preserved goods—chowchow, tomatoes, tomato juice, green beans, beets, pickles, pickled melon, relishes. Two large boxes were filled with bags of homemade potato chips and breads.

Though the Bird-in-Hand Farmers' Market was neither the biggest nor the best known in the area, it was convenient for Mary. In the next hour, we transferred all her goods from the car to a booth in the market. At eight-thirty the doors opened, late for a farmers' market but early for the tourists who often visited it.

"Don't bother coming back for me," Mary said as she accepted money from her first customer. "I'll find a ride home."

I walked around the market enjoying the sights and smells and sounds. The largest crowd stood patiently before the meat counter waiting to buy fresh beef and pork products.

"I just love the ham loaf they sell. It has pork in it as well as the ground ham," said a well-endowed woman with her sunglasses perched on top of her head.

The Mennonite woman standing beside her nodded. "We love the homemade sausage."

A pair of Amish women sat behind a display of hand-braided rugs chatting in "Dutch" as they waited for customers. When I stopped to admire their handiwork, they immediately switched to English.

"May we help you?"

I smiled and shook my head. As I turned away, the women picked up their Dutch conversation where they had dropped it.

It fascinated me that, though basically uneducated, the

Amish were trilingual. At home they spoke their Pennsylvania Dutch dialect, a form of German (*Deutsch* having somewhere through the years become *Dutch*). They spoke English to non-Amish, and High German for religious and ceremonial occasions.

The Zooks, ever gracious, always spoke English in my presence, though on the occasions when I had come home to find a house full of company, they had all been speaking Dutch. As Mary introduced me around, everyone spoke politely in English. As soon as I moved on, the conversations reverted to Dutch.

I wandered out of the farmers' market into the glassware outlet next door. I sighed as I walked carefully between the shelves and tourists. What was I going to do about Todd? I acknowledged what I had known all along: Jake was right. Nice wasn't enough to marry on.

I stopped and looked without seeing at a lovely etched glass tray. Instead I saw Todd's face looking at me critically, thinking love was reforming me into what he thought I should be. Suddenly the image shifted, and I saw Clarke with his dark eyebrows and warm smile. I jerked as though burned.

Murmuring an apology to the three Amish women I bumped into, I hurried outside. To rid my mind of Clarke, I concentrated on the Amish trio. They were going around the store admiring the glassware, chattering in Dutch as they gazed. I doubted the women would buy anything, especially if the jelly jars we drank from at the Zooks' were any indication. Still, beauty could always be admired.

I listened to WJTL—"Worship Jesus the Lord"—as I drove along the Route 30 bypass to Park City Mall just west of

Lancaster. I had been planning this shopping day for a couple of weeks, and I'd been glad to use it as an excuse when Todd asked me to go with him to his family reunion. I flinched at the idea of being introduced to curious and hopeful relatives as "Todd's girl."

My first stop was the Bon Ton where I browsed enviously for a while before going to Sears. I went to the lingerie department and selected a slip with a great froth of lace at the hem. As I waited my turn at the cash register, I stood behind a young Amish girl about Ruth's age, lovely in her prim dress, apron, and head covering. She was buying a slip, panties, and padded bra in a brilliant shade of yellow. I couldn't help but wonder whether she'd hang her purchases on the clothesline with the family's somber clothes or keep them hidden from the eyes of the general populace, especially her mother and father. I suspected the latter.

I drove to Provident Bookstore on my way home, spending time searching for new teaching ideas for kindergarten church. I was the teacher for the month of October, beginning this Sunday, and I felt I hadn't planned my program very well. Perfectionist that I was, I didn't like the unprepared feeling I had. I skimmed several books and decided on three. Only four Sundays but three books. Overkill as usual.

Just before I left, I went to the section where books on counseling and psychology were displayed. Clarke's book was there, prominently promoted under a sign that read "local author." To keep my promise, I bought one.

"Good book," said the woman at the register. "Nice man. My daughter has him for a class at Lancaster Bible College."

"Yes," I said. "He's a personal friend."

I smiled all the way to my car because the woman and her daughter liked Clarke. Stupid.

But Clarke isn't your problem, I reminded myself. Todd is.

I fretted and stewed and prayed as I drove to Rockvale Square, one of the largest outlet malls in the East. As I wandered from store to store and stood in lines to buy what I hoped were really discounted articles, I wrestled with what to do about Todd. In many ways he was my closest friend. The problem was that he didn't want to be my friend, and I now recognized that I didn't want him to be anything else.

"Mom! It's my art teacher!" more than one dumbfounded kid whispered to a harried parent as the afternoon passed. There is something about seeing a teacher in the real world that undoes kids. One of my most vocal and active students stood in line behind me in the Bass shoe store, struck dumb and paralyzed as she held onto her mother's shirt. I smiled at the girl and said, "Hello, Hillary," but she didn't even blink.

"Thank you for being here," her mother said to me. "It's the first time she's been quiet all day."

On my way home I stopped at the Bird-in-Hand bakery, surprised that with the swarm of tourists I actually found a parking place in their tiny lot. I bought a whoopie pie. I got a diet soda (to assuage my guilt over the chocolate-and-white-icing sugar load) and sat in the car to eat and drink. The only thing missing was an Auntie Anne's pretzel. If I was going to ruin my dinner appetite, I might as well do it big time.

I opened today's *Intelligencer Journal* as I chewed and looked at the handsome, photogenic faces of Adam and Irene Hurlbert at a political gala the previous evening. With them was retiring United States Senator Vernon Poltor, broadly smiling his support for Adam.

I was pleased. Each day it appeared more and more certain that the Hurlberts would be in Washington in a matter of weeks. One nice sidelight to Adam's election would be the passing from Lancaster of one Nelson Carmody Hurlbert, age nine. All the more reason to vote in November.

I was almost back to the farm when a car suddenly backed blindly out of a driveway right in front of me. I stomped on the brakes and squealed to a stop inches from its bumper. The young Amish driver screeched off, never even looking my way. A second car followed none too gently, but its driver, another young Amishman with his straw hat pushed back on his head, did remember to look before he roared into the street. He was obviously very unhappy.

With some surprise, I realized I was stopped in front of Aunt Betty Lou and Uncle Bud's house. As I waited for my heart to regain its normal rhythm after the close brush with a collision, I watched Clarke in the driveway talking with yet another Amish boy who climbed into a third car and drove off after his companions.

"Whatever's going on?" I asked as Clarke walked over. Once again, I thought, he sees me at my worst, looking weary and wan at the end of a long day.

"It's the Stoltzfus brothers. They all have cars and keep them hidden in the cornfields most of the time. At least they thought they were hidden." Clarke smiled. "Ammon Stoltzfus is nobody's fool, and he just told his boys to get all the cars off the property. Church is at their house tomorrow, and he doesn't want anyone accidentally finding a car."

"So they parked here?"

"And forgot to ask permission. I guess they figured that anyone with a long driveway wouldn't mind a few extra cars for a night or two. Unfortunately for them, Aunt Betty Lou happened to be looking out the window as they were parking. The boys seemed to have trouble understanding that she wants her drive free for her own guests this evening."

"Are they related to the Stoltzfus boy who was shunned?"

"Cousins. Their uncle would be very upset if he saw those cars. By the way, I've been trying to get hold of you."

I hoped my eyes didn't light up as obviously as I feared they did. "I've been shopping." I indicated the backseat full of packages.

"So I see." He made believe he was counting the packages. "And doing a thorough job of it, too."

"You wanted to talk to me?" I said to divert his attention from my profligacy.

"Right. Aunt Betty Lou decided this morning that she'd like to have one last cookout as the summer fades into memory. She told me to invite someone, so...I know it's very last minute, but can you come to dinner?"

I was inordinately pleased. I hadn't seen Clarke to talk to since the tomato fight and had feared he wasn't interested in me at all. "I'd love to come. Do I have time to go home and change?" I thought of my swirly skirt patterned with reds and purples and jades. I thought of the new red blouse with the voluminous sleeves lying in one of the bags on the back seat. I thought of a hairbrush and toothbrush, rouge and lipstick. "I'm feeling a bit shaggy."

"You look fine to me."

I looked at him, astonished. "I didn't realize you had such a severe vision problem."

He grinned. "I'll walk down for you in thirty minutes. Is that time enough?"

I nodded, stepped on the gas, and went nowhere. I had stalled when I hit the brakes so fast.

"Drat," I muttered, and turned the key in the ignition. Still nothing happened. I looked at the broadly grinning Clarke.

"Put it in park," he said gently.

"Wise guy," I said with no malice. "I'll see you in half an hour."

I drove the short distance to the Zooks', examining the fact that I'd just made a silly mistake in front of Clarke and he didn't seem to mind. He didn't lecture me about how to prevent making a similar mistake again. He didn't laugh. He didn't turn snide.

I could get used to such treatment very easily.

ELEVEN

I watched the last five-year-old race down the hall of the church's educational wing. I'd enjoyed my morning with the kids. Teaching one month a quarter worked well for me. After teaching all week, teaching every Sunday would have been overwhelming. Kindergarten church and its part-time schedule was just right.

I lingered as long as I could, straightening up the already neat shelves of supplies, but when I walked outside, Todd was still waiting for me. My stomach cramped at the sight of him and his I'm-so-glad-to-see-you smile.

In the two weeks since I'd had dinner with Clarke at Aunt Betty Lou's, I'd known it was only a matter of time with Todd. Not that Clarke had asked me to go anywhere else. He hadn't, and maybe he never would. But I had known. After that evening, I had known.

Clarke had walked down to pick me up just as he said. All the Zooks smiled encouragement as we left. Ruth even managed to whisper none too subtly, "Have a wonderful good time, Kristie!"

We walked up the road, enjoying the October sunshine. The first subtle signs of autumn were evident in the wild bitter-sweet berries beginning to pop their golden jackets to reveal their orange undershirts and in the crimson-tipped leaves of the dogwood and the fire bushes. We stopped by a patch of jewelweed, the yellow flowers cheery and the seed pods fat and ready to burst. We touched them and watched as they exploded, curling on themselves and shooting seeds everywhere.

Somehow, by the time we got to Aunt Betty Lou's, we were holding hands. I found his touch unexpectedly intoxicating, tingly. It was all I could do not to burst into song about enchanted evenings and being younger than springtime, the season notwithstanding.

Dinner was delicious, the company more than pleasant, and Clarke attentive. Not look-at-my-girl-isn't-she-wonderful attentive, but still enough to make the evening a delight.

When we left to walk back to the Zooks', I discovered another not-too-subtle sign of fall. It was chilly, and I had neglected to bring a sweater. When I shivered, Clarke couldn't help but notice.

"Let's get you a jacket," he said and led the way to the garage. We climbed the outside stairs to his apartment, and he held the door for me. I looked with interest around his living room as he went to get something for me to slip on.

Neat but beige-bland. A man's apartment.

Suddenly I gasped.

Clarke, coming into the room with a navy sweater in his hands, heard me and smiled. He came up behind me and put his hand on my shoulder.

"Does it look okay there over the sofa?" he asked as we studied my painting, the one bright splash of color in the monochromatic room. In it the Victorian front porch held several fat, white planters with geraniums and ivy tumbling from them. A pair of black-and-white cats lay sleeping on a wicker chair, and a third, a fat, fluffy gray, sat on the top step grooming himself. A red door with a large brass knocker blazed in the otherwise subtle background.

I couldn't stop smiling. "I can't believe it! You shouldn't have! But I'm so glad you did!"

"We said we'd each help the other along. I only kept our bargain. After all, you already had my book."

"Well, sure. And I bought another one. But I know how much this picture cost! There's no comparison."

He shrugged. "You can always go buy lots more books and even us out. I won't stop you."

I spun around and hugged him. "Thank you so much! You don't know what a wonderful gift you've given me."

"Will you hug me like this every time I give you a present?" he asked as he hugged me back. "Or is this only for paintings?"

Anytime, I wanted to say. Anytime at all, gift or no gift.

Instead I unwrapped my arms and turned back to look at the painting. It was just too comfortable with my cheek against his chest. Too intimate. But he kept his arms around me. I leaned back against him, liking very much the sturdy feel of him behind me.

"Do you know I've never seen my work on anyone's wall unless I've given it as a gift?"

"You will. Just give it time. I'm not an art expert by any means—"

"But you know what you like?" I finished.

He laughed. "Well, I do, but I was going to say that you have a very fine sense of color and composition. People will find your work easy to live with."

I sighed with pleasure, and he kissed the top of my head.

He gave me a heavy navy cardigan to slip on for the walk home. It fit somewhat after we rolled the sleeves up several times.

"You're a skinny little thing," he said as he pulled on his jacket.

"Is that good or bad?" I asked. "Not that I can do much about it."

His look from under those dark brows made my breath catch in my throat. "I think you're wonderful just the way you are—skinny, colorful, and charming. I can't imagine you being any more lovely."

I floated all the way home, but I did think it would be a good thing to have a bit of conversation as we walked, so I asked, "How did you come to be involved in counseling?"

He draped his arm casually over my shoulder and said, "It was no great moment of calling, of God's voice in my ear. It was more a matter of getting a sense of what the Word of God can do and wanting others to find the same help there I did. Look." He pointed skyward. "There's the Big Dipper and Orion."

Not to be outdone, I nodded and said, "And there's the Pleiades, the seven sisters, though you can only see six stars. The seventh seems to have disappeared. The seven daughters of Atlas, put into the sky by Zeus."

Clarke stopped and looked at me.

I grinned. "Don't be impressed. I've blown all my astrological knowledge already. I had to do a report once in high school on the constellation Taurus, which the Pleiades are a part of."

"Whew," he said as we resumed walking. "You had me worried. I thought you might be an astronomer as well as an artist."

I laughed at the absurdity of that idea.

"Tell me more about how you became a counselor," I said. "I want to know what made you find such help in the Bible that it led to your life's calling."

He glanced at the sky again. "I already told you about the two years Mom and Dad spent in South America."

I nodded.

"What I didn't mention was how betrayed I felt when they decided to go. It was my junior and senior years in high school, and I took the move as a personal affront. I saw them as ruining my life, and I wasn't the least bit hesitant in telling them." He looked at me. "It's still embarrassing to realize how selfish and petty I was."

I shrugged. "It's the age. So what happened?"

"I refused to go with them. Obviously I couldn't stay in New York alone, so I came to live with Uncle Bud and Aunt Betty Lou, which I hardly saw as an improvement over Brazil. And I went to church and youth group regularly because in their house there wasn't a choice. At first I was so mad at God that I must have been a festering thorn in everyone's side. But gradually God broke through my hurt, and I committed my life to him. After all, who else even cared about me?

"I was still mad at Mom and Dad. When I thought about them, it was, 'Well, God, at least you love me.' Then one morning I was reading my Bible and I read Philippians 4:11: 'I have learned to be content whatever the circumstances.' I realized I had to learn to be content with a dad who put a career move before his son and a mom who supported that move. I had to choose. I realized I had to learn to be content in quiet, provincial Bird-in-Hand, hardly the exciting place that New York had been. There was the apostle Paul sitting in jail, being content. If he could do it, so could I. It was what God wanted, and I chose to learn what God wanted."

He glanced down at me. "That was the start of realizing how practical the Word of God is and how it can affect lives. By the time I visited my parents during the summer before my senior year, I was a different person from the nasty, grumpy, self-absorbed kid they left behind. I even realized that Dad would have been crazy to turn down that job. When I came back to Bird-in-Hand for my senior year, it wasn't to spite my parents but because I wanted to continue with the friendships and stuff around here.

"I also learned to trust that verse my senior year in college when I got mono so badly that I lost a semester and didn't graduate with my class."

We climbed the front stairs at the Zooks' and turned to face each other.

"Thanks for telling me that story," I said. "Now I know why your book is so practical."

"Yeah, I tend to be practical rather than philosophical."

"Sort of like an engineer instead of a scientist."

"I never heard anyone put it that way before, but that's about it. A theological engineer."

When he cupped the side of my face, stared at me yet again and said, "Good night, Kristie. I couldn't have asked for a better evening," I floated upstairs.

It wasn't until a couple of days later that I realized he hadn't said anything about a repeat date. And he hadn't called or stopped since. I knew there was a chance that he might never come for me again, that he had been as caught by the magic of the evening as I, nothing more. Even so, I knew what I had to do about Todd.

Lord, I called silently as I stood in the church parking lot looking into the smiling face of this man who would be my love. *The right words? Please?*

Todd was obviously delighted to see me. "Hey, Kristie. How were the little devils this morning?"

"Fine."

"I envied them, spending that time with you while I had to sit alone in church. Where shall we go to eat?"

I clutched my papers and workbooks to my chest and studied the toes of my boots.

"Kristie?" Todd's voice was uncertain. "What's wrong?"

I took a deep breath. "No, Todd." And I reached for my car door handle.

He touched my arm. I looked up and saw confusion and something else—fear?—in his face.

"No what?" he asked. "No, you have other plans? No, we can't do anything today?"

"No to both," I said. I forced my eyes to stay steady on his. "No, I have no other plans, but no, not today."

He looked at me silently, thoughtfully, sadly. "Tomorrow? Next weekend?"

I shook my head.

"Ever again?"

My eyes fell before the pain in his. I whispered, "No," as I leaned against my yellow car for support. I felt like an airline official telling the waiting relatives there were no survivors.

"Why?" Todd asked. "What happened? What have I done?"

This was every bit as bad as I'd feared, and my voice shook as I answered.

"You haven't done anything, Todd. You're a very nice guy. I like you a lot, but—" How could I explain to him something I could barely articulate to myself? I cleared my throat.

"I know you care for me, Todd. Or you care for who you think I could or should be. But I'm not who you want me to be. I'm just me, and I can't be anyone else. I don't want to be anyone else. And too much about me—my weaknesses and peculiarities and independent spirit—bothers you too much."

"But—" The lawyer in him was ready to argue, but I plowed on.

"It's just not sensible to continue a relationship where there's such a basic clash of personalities. And that's the way it is with us, whether you admit it or not. I want someone who will accept me the way I am, painting, yellow car, Amish farm, and all. I want someone who doesn't get embarrassed when I burst into song. And you...you need someone who will cherish your guidance, not bristle under it."

I watched his eyes widen in denial and silently entreated him to understand what I was trying to say.

He studied my face intently, making me feel like a sloppy Marine at inspection. "Jon Clarke," he finally said. "It's him, isn't it? Don't think I haven't noticed how he watches you."

He does? He watches me? My heart soared, but I forced myself not to show my elation.

"And don't think," Todd continued, "that I'm unaware that he took you to dinner at his aunt and uncle's. You wouldn't go to my family reunion, but you had dinner with Clarke's family, and on the same day."

Oops. Word certainly got around.

He turned and leaned against the car next to me, as though he couldn't look at me any more. It hurt too much.

"And you know what?" He ran his hand through his curls. "I can't even get mad at him or you because I like him too. Always have, from back when he finished high school here."

He looked at me, curls sproinging, eyes sad. "It is Jon Clarke, isn't it?" he repeated.

I blinked. "No—Yes—I don't know," I stammered. "I honestly don't, Todd. But I wouldn't be thinking about him at all if I loved you the way you want me to."

"Maybe you just haven't given yourself enough time."

Talk about grasping at straws! I shook my head. "No. I think two years is enough time. Don't you?"

"Kristie, please."

"No. Because you don't really love me," I said. "At least, not the real me. I'm sorry, Todd." I smiled weakly, turned, and fumbled my way into the car.

Only when I began to back from my parking place did he rouse himself. He walked away slowly, shoulders drooping. I felt so guilty!

My guilt at being a heartbreaker didn't last long. By the time I reached the farm, I felt marvelous, light and unencumbered. I truly felt bad about hurting Todd, but I was so sure I was right that I felt butterfly free.

As I hung up my garnet, green, and navy slubbed-silk blazer, I sang snatches of whatever came to mind, changing the lyrics to fit my mood. I pulled on my comfortable turquoise-and-black sweats, and was glad there was no one home but me. I could rejoice as loudly as I pleased.

Glory, glory, hallelujah.
Glory, glory, hallelujah.
Glory, glory, hallelujah!
I'm free! I'm free! I'm free!

I took The Key from my bureau and slipped it into the pocket of my sweatshirt. Maybe today was the day I should take charge everywhere. Maybe I'd visit Mr. Geohagan and make him take The Key back whether he wanted to or not.

Fat chance. I'd probably be carrying the thing around when I was an old lady and he was a wizened, desiccated mummy. Still, I had more than enough to sing about as I puttered around Mary's empty kitchen making some lunch.

"I'd say you're having a good day," said Jake from his doorway. "You've been singing like a demented bird."

I spun around. "Jake! You're sneaking again. And I am having a wonderful day! I made a momentous decision, and I'm relieved, relieved, relieved!" I threw my arms wide and spun in a circle.

He shook his head at my excesses. "So what happened? You quit your job? You're getting married? You hit it big in the lottery?" He rolled across the room, and I poured him a Coke.

"Need a sandwich?" I asked.

He shook his head. "You sold a painting?"

"Did I tell you Clarke bought one?"

"Several times. Has another sold?"

"Don't I wish. You'll never guess. I said farewell to my 'good friend' Todd."

Jake looked at me with a smug smile. "I knew it all along."

"Sure you did."

"Well, let's say I hoped it all along. I like Jon Clarke too."

I put up my hand. "No conclusion jumping, please. Clarke and I are merely good friends."

He nodded. "And you're hard on good friends. I'd better warn him."

I put away the lunch things and tidied up the kitchen. I wouldn't want Mary to find it different from the way she'd left it.

"Want to go for a ride?" Jake asked, indicating his van in the drive. "I'm going whether you come or not, but it'd be fun to have company."

I accepted readily. "This is freedom day. We'll celebrate my release and your independence."

We settled in the van and Jake said, "I can't tell you how good it feels to drive again, to take myself somewhere instead of being taken."

His hands were steady and certain on the controls, and he hummed tunelessly as he drove. I leaned back in my seat and watched the glory of autumn in the golden oaks and brilliant sugar maples.

Jake blew his horn suddenly and waved.

"Aunt Naomi's," he explained. "That's where Mom and Father and Elam are visiting."

"You didn't want to go?"

"I feel uncomfortable when it's meeting Sunday and I know everyone's thinking that I wasn't there and I should have been."

I nodded. I could understand that. "Where's Ruth?"

"She and Isaiah went away for the weekend."

"Isaiah?"

"Isaiah Beiler, her boyfriend. I think they're going to get married."

"I thought boyfriends were kept secret until the engagement was announced."

"Sometimes, and sometimes it's like Ruth and Isaiah. They've been going together for two years. How can you hide that when everybody in the group knows everybody else?"

I smiled at a tangle of goldenrod and milkweed growing at the road's edge. "Well, where did Ruth and Isaiah go?"

"To the Poconos with Dan Beiler, Isaiah's brother, and his girlfriend."

"Is Dan English, so he can drive them?"

Jake smiled crookedly. "No, he's Amish. He just hasn't joined the church yet. He keeps his car in a rented garage in town."

"And Isaiah?"

"I predict this fall."

"Just like Ruth and Elam?"

"You have to join to get married."

"Elam's getting married? I didn't even know he had a girl!"

"Not Elam! Ruth and Isaiah. Up till now Isaiah's stayed free of church discipline. He's always intended to be Amish. He's just been enjoying his rumschpringes, usually with my sister."

"Oh, Jake, surely not!" I was appalled at the implications of his comment.

"Oh yes. Last fall Isaiah drove when they rented a trailer and took a long trip to New England."

"Just Isaiah and Ruth?"

"And Joe Lapp and his girl."

I was stunned. "And your parents let her go?"

"You can be certain that Mom and Father don't like these little jaunts—and the frequent overnights—but they're afraid that if they make a fuss, they'll lose her like they did Andy and Zeke and me."

Jake smiled at my consternation and confusion. "You've got to remember, Kristie, that there are two types of Amish, religious and cultural. My parents are religious Amish. They love God and believe the church's teachings. They live by the Ordnung because they believe it's the avenue to eternal life, and they want eternal life."

I nodded as we drove past six barrel-chested work horses placidly eating grass in a field.

He continued. "Ruth and Isaiah are Amish because that's the life they've been raised to live. Their families and friends live that way, so they do too. But the outer form has no inner significance."

"I understand. There are people like your parents and people like Ruth and Isaiah in my church too. Even the Bible talks about people who have the form of faith but not the substance."

Jake nodded, relieved that I understood.

"What about Elam?" I asked. I liked that intense young man.

"For a while I thought he was doing what he thought he had to do to please Father, but lately I've begun to think he's becoming a religious Amish. He drinks some, but basically I'd say he's very moral. He seems to be looking for more than the outer trappings. I've even found him reading the Bible, something many Amishmen never do. And in English, no less! He said he wanted to understand it."

"Many Amish people never read the Bible?"

Jake looked at me. "Especially in English. Interesting group, my people, aren't they? Their major consistency is inconsistency."

"Well, what about you, Jake? Where do you see yourself?"

"Good question." His voice turned melancholy. "I think I feel in between. I'm not Amish, but I'm not a Christian like you and Jon Clarke. I'm not sick with germs and all, but I'm not well. I'm not ignorant or dumb, but I'm not educated. I'm in between—and it's a very lonely place to be."

On this somber note, we arrived back at the farm.

"You go on in," Jake said. "I'm going to stay out here and feel sorry for myself for a while."

"Jake, don't."

"See you, Kristie."

As I climbed reluctantly out of the van, he turned the radio to a rock station and adjusted the volume to a level guaranteed to damage his hearing. The sound followed me into the house, muted only when I closed the door.

I told myself that the worst thing I could do for Jake was to think, *Poor Jake,* yet I found myself thinking exactly that as I crossed the great room and started up the stairs. I was so lost in thought that I misjudged my step, stubbing my toe and barking my shin.

"Drat!" I said as I rubbed the painful areas.

Immediately a loud crash sounded upstairs, and Big Bird began to squawk. Simultaneously heavy footfalls slapped across the floor.

I froze in surprise and fear, memories of that night at Mr.

Geohagan's crowding in. My eyes were on the door to my rooms. No one was even supposed to be in the house, let alone in my rooms.

Suddenly a man I'd never seen before burst into view and stared menacingly down the stairs at me.

My stomach lurched. He was so big! And he looked so threatening with his Braves baseball cap pulled down over his forehead and his gloved fists balled.

He never hesitated. "Out of my way, girl!" he yelled and charged straight at me.

I screamed, and the sound ricocheted madly off the walls. There was no room in the narrow stairwell for him to pass me. We were going to collide, and such a collision seemed to be his intended purpose as he raced directly at me.

I have no recollection of being pushed or falling, but given my skinny body and his considerable bulk, I must have gone flying. Suddenly I was lying in a heap at the base of the stairs as the man climbed none too gently over me. I'm sure he wasn't wearing hobnailed boots, but it certainly felt like it. I put my hands to my face and curled into a ball to protect myself. I stayed that way until I heard the door slam and the man race across the porch.

I uncurled cautiously and looked at the door, then breathed a great sigh as I confirmed that he was truly gone. Slowly I pulled myself up and limped to the door. I must have hit my hip on the stairs as I fell; it was already stiff. Or maybe he kicked me as he passed. Sore toe, scraped shin, and bruised hip. Not bad for less than one minute of time.

I was uncertain what to do. I could call the police, but somehow the idea of the police at Mary and John's house was unthinkable. Flashing lights and guns just didn't fit here. In fact, this peaceful Amish farm made the violence of the big man and my feelings of violation all the more intense.

I closed my eyes and tried to picture the intruder. Nothing. All I saw was a big man, a terrifying man, rushing at me. The only thing I was certain of was that he wasn't Amish, and I didn't even know why I was so sure of that fact beyond the baseball cap.

I stepped cautiously outside. No one was visible out front but Jake, sitting in his van with his back to the house, lost in his music. There were no cars or people on the road, and I wondered where Hawk was. There's never a biting dog around when you need one.

I limped to the far end of the porch and peered through the wisteria vine. A bulky figure in a baseball cap was running through the corn stubble toward the Stoltzfus farm. It was my giant of an intruder, looking oddly small in the distance.

Well, at least he was gone. I limped back into the house, rubbing my sore hip.

"Quiet down, Big Bird," I called. "I'm coming."

I went upstairs one step at a time and found my room almost the way I'd left it except for my philodendron lying on the floor in a tangle of leaves, soil, and pottery shards. Obviously that was the loud crash I'd heard. I'd been afraid it was Big Bird and his cage. My clothing on the pegs was askew, the items on my night table slightly awry, my bureau top rearranged, but nothing seemed harmed. I checked carefully, but I could find nothing missing.

It wasn't until I began cleaning up the plant that I discovered my cell phone under the mess, its casing cracked and dirt lodged in every crevice. Obviously I wouldn't be talking to anyone on it ever again.

"In fact," I said to Jake later as I stood beside the van, "I can think of no reason why anyone would try and rob the farm.

This isn't a place where there's money, is it?"

Jake shook his head. "Father keeps all his money in the bank. He's very smart financially, and he'd never leave anything lying around. Your TV's still there?"

I nodded.

"Let me check the rest of the house to see if anything's gone. I've got several electronic things I'd hate to lose." He pushed the proper buttons and lowered his chair to the ground.

"Why would anyone risk coming here in the middle of the afternoon?" I asked as I walked to the house with him. I didn't want to be alone.

"Who's usually here on most Sunday afternoons, Kristie? Mom and Father visit family. You're out with Todd. No one's here but me, and I'm no great threat. Conveniently, even I went out today. If you look at it from the least chance of being caught, Sunday afternoon's it."

"But why take the risk at all?" I asked.

Jake shook his head. "We have little to steal, that's for sure. How about you? You're not keeping a stash of valuable jewels up there, are you? He was in your room."

I grinned weakly. "Only the few diamonds and rubies I've been able to buy with the overwhelming income from my paintings," I said, digging my shaking hands into my sweatshirt pocket. I began fiddling with The Key. "I've got nothing. Nothing."

TWELVE

When Mary, John, and Elam returned, I was just getting into my car to go to the hospital. I climbed out, said hello, and told them about our afternoon visitor. Predictably they were distressed, but they were relieved that I hadn't called the police.

"You chust be wery careful, Kristie. We don't want nothing happening to you," John said as he and Elam went to the barn to feed the animals and milk the cows.

"Don't worry. I'll take care," I said, touched by his concern. I smiled reassuringly at Mary. "I'm on my way to visit Mr. Geohagan. Tonight's his last night at the hospital. Tomorrow he gets transferred to Holiday House."

Mary nodded approval. "I know that place. My cousin Sadie Lapp who's church Amish had to go there when all her family died. It's nice for that kind of place. It's run by the Mennonites. They're wonderful at taking care of people."

Too bad Mr. Geohagan couldn't talk to Mary. He didn't see his move so positively.

"Holiday House," he'd complained. "What kind of asinine name is that for a nursing home? Like it's only open on Christmas and Thanksgiving and the rest of the year they park me in the street. Or do they think that a gooey name is going to make me happy to go there? I may be sick, but that doesn't mean I can't think. Hopeless House is more like it. Or Humiliation House. Or Heartache House. Or Hateful House."

"What do you do?" I asked to cut off his tirade. "Spend all

your time looking for alliteration?"

He stared at me, steely eyed. "Hell House is my favorite."

Poor, lonely man...but a lonely man who must have the best supplemental insurance policy in the world to afford being in the hospital this long.

I had just waved good-bye to Mary and had my car door open when Clarke pulled into the Zooks' drive.

"Hi," I called and waved, shutting the door.

"Hi, yourself," he said as he walked over. "Are you coming or going?"

Whew, was he handsome! I was mesmerized by his smile, his eyes, his gait, his everything. I hoped I didn't look as infatuated as I felt. After all, I was a long way from sweet sixteen. Sorry, Mr. G. I think I'll just see you tomorrow.

"She's going," said Jake, who had rolled up silently beside me. "She's going to visit Mr. Geohagan and be Lady Bountiful, whoever she was."

"Jake!" I exclaimed angrily.

Both men looked at me, Clarke surprised by the vehemence in my voice, Jake delighted with himself, knowing he'd gotten to me. To cover my outburst I said quietly and reasonably, "Jake, you're sneaking again." I turned to Clarke. "His chair doesn't make noise. I think he oils the wheels."

"I bet the hospital's noisy though, isn't it? Poor Mr. Geohagan." Jake said with mock pity. "He needs you."

"You've been very faithful in visiting him, Kristie," said Clarke, watching with interest and probably understanding as I shot daggers at Jake, who was grinning like an idiot. "I hope he appreciates you."

"I think he does." I said, wondering what people would think of someone who beat up a wheelchair-bound man. "I keep praying that my kindness will let him accept God's love.

He's absolutely furious with God about his wife and daughter."

"It's funny," said Jake, suddenly serious, "but I never considered blaming God for my accident. I may not know much about the deeper things of life, but I have noticed that tragedies seem to strike both the godly and the ungodly without favoritism. I get mad at being crippled because obviously I'd rather be walking, but it's the guy who ran the stop sign that I get mad at, not God."

"The thing that fascinates me is that Mr. Geohagan blames God rather than himself or Cathleen," said Clarke. "He seems to conveniently forget that choices always have consequences."

I agreed. "That's my thought, too. There they all were, living without a single thought for God and in defiance of his standards. Then when the natural consequences of their acts occurred, suddenly it's all God's fault." I shook my head. "And believe me, Mr. Geohagan can be very brutal and caustic about it all."

"And you keep going back to that?" asked Jake.

"Why not?" I shrugged. "He needs me."

"But how much do you owe to a quarrelsome old man you met in the emergency room?"

"If I don't go visit, who will? Besides, he's not quarrelsome; he's sad. And I have The Key."

Immediately I realized what I'd said. *Tell no one! Promise!* I made a face and muttered under my breath.

"What's wrong?" Clarke asked.

"Nothing."

"Nothing?"

"Nothing."

"Then why do you look so guilty?"

"I do?"

"You do."

The curse of an honest face. "I just broke a promise."

"About what?" Jake asked.

Clarke looked at me closely. "About a key?"

"I'm not supposed to tell anyone I have it."

"Why not?"

"Mr. Geohagan told me not to."

"Why?"

"I have no idea."

"Let me get this straight," Clarke said. "You have Mr. Geohagan's key, and you're not supposed to tell anyone you have it, but you don't know why."

I nodded. "That's it."

"Why did he give it to you in the first place?" Jake asked.

"Because he might die?" I said.

Clarke laughed, and his eyes crinkled almost shut. "Don't ask us, Kristie. We're asking you."

I grinned back at him, the tension draining away and my shoulders relaxing. It was too late to worry about saying too much now.

"Mr. Geohagan gave me the key the day we met in the ER. I think he thought he might die, and he gave it to me for safe-keeping. He even wrote instructions before he had bypass surgery, leaving the key to me. I've tried to give it back to him several times, but he keeps telling me he wants me to hold it for him."

"What kind of a key is it?" asked Jake. "A house key? A car key? A safe-deposit box key? A treasure-chest key?"

"I don't know." I pulled it from my jacket pocket and held it out in my palm.

"Looks like a regular house key to me," said Jake.

"It's pretty small for that. Maybe a garage key?" I had studied the little piece of metal so many times. "All I know is that it isn't his front-door key because he gave me another one when I went to his apartment."

"Too bad it wasn't a closet key," said Clarke with a wicked smile.

I made a face at him and dropped the key into my purse. "I'll have to tell him that I told you two."

"He won't mind," said Clarke.

"I hope not."

I parked my car as close to the hospital entrance as I could, which wasn't very close since the whole world seemed to be visiting this particular hospital on this particular night. I squared my shoulders, confident I'd find Mr. Geohagan in a foul mood because of tomorrow's move. Wait until he heard my confession.

"I must tell you something," I said hesitantly as I sat in the chair beside his bed. I forced myself to stop twisting my hands like a nervous old lady and stuffed them into my sweatshirt pockets to keep them apart. "I told some people about your key today. I didn't mean to. It just sort of slipped out. I'm sorry."

"Who?" he asked immediately, warily, his frown intense.

"A son of the Amish family I'm living with and a friend of his."

Mr. Geohagan relaxed visibly at that information and actually made an attempt at a smile. "Don't worry about it. I'm certain there's no harm done."

I felt great relief. "But I don't want to keep the key anymore."

"I'd feel better if you did."

I shook my head as I pulled my hand out of my pocket. I

reached out and put the key on his night table. It clinked quietly.

"Have you got some nasty relative who's after the fortune it unlocks or something?" I grinned.

He didn't grin back.

I felt a chill. I looked at him lying there defenseless and incapacitated. I looked at the key, lowercase now that it wasn't my responsibility. Maybe I should keep it after all if it made him happy. I reached for it.

"Hey, Mr. Geohagan!"

I jumped and turned at the loud voice, key forgotten.

In walked an aide with a small tray. She smiled so broadly her gums showed. "How are you doing tonight?"

"How do you think?" he asked sourly.

She ignored his snarl. "I've got a snack for you, Mr. Geohagan." She set down the tray that held a ginger ale and a cupcake, then rolled the tray over the bed. "I bet you'll enjoy it. You'd better. I baked that cupcake just for you as a going-away present."

"Hah!" he said with considerable force. "I haven't enjoyed any food here yet, and I'm not starting now, especially if you baked it."

The aide left with a huge smile on her face.

"She drives me crazy," Mr. Geohagan said to me. "Everything I say or do makes her laugh."

"But that was nice of her to bring you this cupcake."

He snorted again. "She didn't do it for me. She did it for herself. She's a do-gooder."

"Like me?" I asked with asperity.

"No," he said. "You're cute."

I just shook my head. "And you're impossible."

I watched as he picked the cupcake to death, eating every single crumb but slowly, slowly so I wouldn't think he was enjoying it. The key lay forgotten. I didn't remember it again until I was walking across the parking lot and reached in my voluminous shoulder bag for the ignition key, which was hiding as usual.

I made a face. Should I go back to the room and get it? What could happen to it overnight?

Tomorrow, I told myself. I'll get it tomorrow.

I grabbed one strap of my shoulder bag with my left hand and pulled it open with my right, peering hopefully into the dark interior, willing my car keys to walk to the surface of the collection within.

So quickly I didn't have time to react, a man's hand grabbed my bag, pulling on it with a force that threw me off balance. At the same time his other hand shoved me hard in the middle of my back, sending me reeling.

Attacked twice in one day! I thought as I fell. Not fair!

As I went down, some instinct kept my hands clamped to my purse rather than reaching out to break my fall. Nobody was going to get my things, not if I had anything to say about it! I had no idea of half the stuff that was in my bag, but I knew I didn't want some stranger pawing through any of it.

Don't let him get it, Lord!

I twisted slightly midair so that I landed on my side rather than my face, and my twisting broke the thief's hold. It was either let go or fall with me. I hit the ground in a bone-crunching thud, bounced a time or two, and through the daze of pain rolled protectively onto my stomach, my purse beneath me.

I took a deep breath and tried to scream, but only a gurgle emerged.

I sensed more than heard that my attacker was gone, and I slowly, painfully began pulling myself to my feet by using my car door handle. A small crowd converged on me about the time I got to my knees and helped me the rest of the way up. I looked gratefully at a security guard, an orderly, and two other men, who were apparently visitors too.

"Are you all right?"

"Did he get your purse?"

"Uh-oh. Look at your leg. Blood."

"How's your head? Can you tell me your name? Should you be standing?" The last was from the orderly.

I was grateful for the strong arms supporting me, because once again my own knees weren't up to the job.

"He's gone, isn't he?" I managed to whisper.

"So quick you wouldn't believe it!" said security. "He had a car waiting just over there." He pointed to the edge of the lot. "Let's get you inside so they can check you over."

"I'm fine," I insisted. "Really, I'm fine." Fortunately none of my rescuers listened.

They shepherded me into the ER, the two strangers making a seat for me with clasped hands. The orderly walked beside us, reaching over to take my pulse. The security guard scurried ahead to open the door with great dramatic flair, an unnecessary act since the door was automatic, but it seemed to make him feel better.

I clutched at the guy on my left to keep from sliding off my perch as they slued sideways to fit through the door without missing a step. My purse, still slung over my shoulder, bumped rhythmically against the one man's side as the orderly led us through the waiting room into the treatment area. Harriet wasn't on duty tonight, and neither was the sad nurse or absentminded doctor.

An hour later, I was finally alone. I ached and knew that tomorrow I'd be black-and-blue all down my right side. I'd landed on the same spot on my hip as when I tumbled down the steps earlier in the afternoon. My shoulder was stiff and tender, but an X-ray showed nothing was broken. My right hand, arm, and leg were painted bright red where I had brush burns, and there was a good-sized lump above my right temple where my head had bounced on the macadam.

A policeman had patiently taken my tale, but both he and I knew that nothing would come of the report. I'd seen no one, and I didn't even know why I felt so certain it was a man who had pushed me. The one positive thing was that when I took inventory of my bag, nothing was missing. I even found the car keys.

Now I sat on a bench and waited for Clarke to come and get me. The doctor had insisted that I not drive home because of the lump on my head.

"You have a slight concussion," he said. "You mustn't risk getting dizzy while driving."

Just last week—just yesterday—I would have called Todd. In all honesty and from sheer habit, he still would have been easiest to call even now, but it wouldn't be fair to him. I had removed him from the place in my life where he was that special person to call on in trouble. I had to leave it that way, even if calling Clarke felt like imposing.

Poor Clarke. Always escorting me to and from hospitals.

Drained, I closed my eyes to rest. I opened them some time later to find Clarke sitting beside me.

"He didn't mind," I said.

"I beg your pardon?"

"Mr. Geohagan. He didn't mind that I told you and Jake about the key."

"Hang Mr. Geohagan," said Clarke with feeling. "How are you?"

"Fine." I smiled weepily. "They just won't let me drive."

He smiled back and pushed my bangs aside. "From the looks of you, they were right. I'm glad you called."

"Poor Clarke. You probably won't believe this, but I'm not accident prone."

He slid his arm around my waist and led me to his car. Unfortunately it was parked right outside the emergency area. I would have preferred a longer walk to enjoy his comfort and concern.

The evening was warm and velvety, the light soft. I rested my head against the back of the seat and relaxed as he drove out of town, heading for the farm.

"There are a lot of buggies out tonight," I said as we waited for a break in traffic to pass one.

"Families returning from social visits and young people going to sings." Clarke passed one buggy only to find himself behind another. "Do you feel well enough to take a little drive?"

"I think so." As long as it's with you. "Where to?"

"Over 23 to Morgantown and down 10 toward Honey Brook."

"As long as I don't have to move, it sounds fine."

He turned at Smoketown to take the back roads to 23. "Poor Kristie. Beaten up by a dog and thieves. Did he get anything?"

"No. When I fell, I rolled onto my bag and started screaming." I smiled when I recalled the thin stream of sound that had pushed its way passed my closed throat. "At least I tried to scream. He didn't have time to get anything. My heroes chased him away."

I realized that as I talked I had picked up my purse from the floor and put it on my lap, arms wrapped around it. I returned it to the floor.

"Not that he'd have gotten much. I'm sort of a magpie when

it comes to my purse. A bunch of dirty Kleenexes, empty Life Savers wrappers, deposit slips, a couple of Magic Markers, and a small sketch pad. Stuff like that. Still, I'd have hated to replace the credit cards and license and Social Security card."

We were silent for a while, and then I asked, "Have you ever been robbed?"

"Not personally, like having my pocket picked, but we were robbed when I was about thirteen. We came home from vacation to find the house ransacked. I lost a magnificent coin collection my grandfather had given me shortly before he died. It was underinsured, but it wasn't the monetary loss that hurt. They took something very special to me, and I remember how bad I felt. It was like Grandpop being taken twice. Thieves are cruel in a way they probably don't even consider."

I nodded as we turned south onto 10 and immediately wished I hadn't. My head swam. I closed my eyes and rested my head on the headrest.

Soon Clarke said, "Look."

Directly ahead of us was a line of buggies, the line broken here and there by cars slowly weaving their way through the pack. Clarke began the passing and waiting game too.

"I've never seen so many," I said, sitting up, delighted. "There must be fifty or sixty of them."

All the buggies were open two seaters. In some, two young men rode, in others couples sat shoulder to shoulder. But what delighted me most were the double-dating couples. One boy and girl sat conventionally, but the second couple sat on their laps, the boy on the boy and the girl on the girl. The topmost boy handled the reins.

All the girls were prim and correct, with their shawls draped over their shoulders against the growing chill of the evening, and dark bonnets over their organdy kapps. The young men, hats firm on their Dutch-boy haircuts, proudly drove their best horses. Couples called from buggy to buggy as they drove, laughing and joking together.

The long line crested a hill, and I watched as buggy after buggy turned into one farm lane.

"I've heard of buggy jams before, especially around Intercourse on a Saturday night, but I've never seen a procession like this." I couldn't stop smiling. "And I love the double dates!"

"I thought you would."

As I watched the buggies, I tried to reconcile the other-world appearance of innocence with what I knew to be reality. These Amish kids were like any other group of kids. Some came from fine families, some from hypocritical families, some from strong families, some from fearful families. And appearances to the contrary, they were being touched more and more by modern technology. Some even belonged to spas and pumped iron.

"You know," I said, "while I don't agree with the Amish way of life, I hate the thought that it might pass away. It's so fascinating!"

Clarke grinned. "You sound like a sociologist. Just never forget that Christ died to release us from bondage to the law, whether it's the Mosaic law or the Ordnung."

Suddenly I realized we were approaching the twin hills south of Honey Brook, the place where Jake had had his accident. I sat up straight and watched as Clarke's headlights picked out the intersection where someone had run a stop sign and changed a young man's life forever.

"This is the spot," I said. Clarke nodded. He slowed as if in respect for Jake.

"Look!" I grabbed his arm and pointed.

There beside the road, just visible in the dusk, was a little white cross, the kind people sometimes put to mark a place where a loved one has been killed. I stared at the little marker on which hung a small wreath decorated with a gold bow and gold flowers.

"Someone else was in an accident here," I whispered. "And whoever it was must have died."

I felt Clarke glance at me, and I smiled reassuringly. He reached out and softly touched my cheek.

"Why don't you take tomorrow off to recuperate?" he suggested when we arrived back at the farm. "Uncle Bud and I will see to it that your car is back by tomorrow evening. Okay?"

"Thanks," I said. Even though I was feeling pretty much back to normal—if I didn't turn my head too quickly or try to raise my arm above my shoulder or put all my weight on my right hip and leg—I knew school would be more than I could handle. "You're a good doctor, Dr. Griffin."

I reached out impulsively and hugged him. I was more than pleased when he returned the embrace with enthusiasm.

THIRTEEN

I set my easel so I had a fine view of the brook that ran through the patch of woods on the acreage down the road from the house. As I prepared to paint, filling my water bottle from the brook, taping my paper in place, preparing my palette, I despaired of catching the glorious oranges and reds of the sugar maples. They burned with an intensity that was hot to the eye. How could I translate that onto paper?

In the small brook there was a pool no more than five feet by five feet, but on its smooth surface floated layers of fiery leaves. I planned to paint the pool and the delicate cascade that fed it. I could use the white of the paper for the rapids and as a foil to the steel blue of the water. And that marvelous brilliance of the leaves! Sorrel and cinnamon and scarlet, cadmium and crimson and gold. What a wonderful challenge.

I began to work, frowning with effort and smiling with pleasure at the same time.

Some time later the snap of a twig brought my head up. How long had I been painting? I rubbed the back of my neck and looked toward the road and the sound.

A man stood watching me.

My skin began to crawl. True, he looked harmless enough in khaki cords and a navy sweater, but I felt threatened.

"Nice picture," he said as he walked toward me.

I nodded, watching warily. I knew that he couldn't begin to see the painting from his angle and distance.

"I saw you painting when I drove by, and I had to stop. I've always wanted to know how a person paints." When I was noncommittal, he moved closer. "What's the first step? Do you start from the top and work down or what?"

"The background comes first with watercolors," I said hesitantly even as a shout cut across my comment.

"Come on, Kristie! It's time to go!"

Thank you, Lord!

"That's Jake," I announced. "He's come for me. I have to go."

I got up quickly from my camp stool. I knew my relief must be obvious to the man, but uncharacteristically I didn't care. I gathered my supplies, hurrying to get away from this man who inexplicably bothered me so. I dumped my water, stuffed the used paper towels into a plastic bag, threw the paint tubes into their box. I collapsed my easel, telescoping its legs and stashing it in my canvas bag.

As I threw the bag over my shoulder and held my painting carefully flat in front of me, I glanced at the stranger.

He wasn't there. I looked around in surprise. Sure enough, the woods were empty. With an eerie, unsettled feeling, I hurried to Jake's van.

"Who was that?" Jake asked, pointing to a car disappearing over the crest of the hill.

"I don't know. He said he saw me working and stopped because he wanted to know how I painted."

"He saw you painting?"

"That's what he said."

"From the road?"

I nodded.

Jake shook his head. "You can't see the brook from the road. The underbrush is too thick. Even I couldn't see you, and I knew you were there. That's why I yelled."

I looked back the way I'd just come. My spine prickled

again as I saw that Jake was right. No casual driver could ever have seen me. The man had known I was there and had sought me out.

But why?

"Did you see what he looked like?" I asked.

He shrugged. "Just a man in a Braves cap."

My mouth suddenly went dry. "A Braves cap?" I whispered. "That's what the other man wore."

Jake looked at me, concern all over his face. "The one who pushed you down the stairs?"

I nodded. "This is creepy. And scary!"

To distract myself, I reached to adjust my watercolor as it lay on the floor behind me. The brook pleased me, as did the little waterfall that fed it. "I'm not sure about the leaves," I said. "Are the colors strong enough?"

Jake looked behind him. "They look great to me, but I'm no expert. I only—"

"—know what I like," I finished for him.

He laughed and patted my hand. "You've got me pegged."

As we started down the road, my mind glommed on to the man in the Braves cap. Jake glanced at me.

"Kristie, it's okay. Don't worry about him." I felt comforted until he continued, "Though I'm glad we'd made plans for me to pick you up."

During the drive to White Horse and the farm auction, I forced myself to relax. I was here in the van and the man wasn't. I was safe. Besides, I couldn't do anything about him anyway because I couldn't swear he was the man I'd seen in the house. The man today hadn't touched me, hadn't been anything but polite. You can't turn a man in to the authorities because he makes you feel creepy.

By the time Jake became embroiled in the minor traffic jam

of cars, buggies, and horse-drawn wagons jockeying for position in the barnyard in White Horse, I no longer felt threatened. I was too fascinated by everything around me.

Jake managed to get a parking place near the drive and next to a wagon loaded with a refrigerator, a treadle sewing machine, a double bedstead, a kitchen table, and five mismatched chairs. I watched in fascination as a red-bearded Amishman and his young son maneuvered a bureau and a rocking chair onto the already overloaded wagon and lashed everything into place.

Jake watched them with a cocked eyebrow. "So Red Daniel is buying furniture. I wonder which of his girls is getting married? Poor man's got six daughters and only Little Daniel."

"What's so bad about six daughters?" I challenged.

"A lot in a culture that looks on unmarried women as not fulfilled. A spinster aunt is always treated nicely, and sometimes she even has a little home of her own. She might get a job as a housekeeper or work in a shop or teach to support herself. But still, unmarried women depend on their fathers. Red Daniel doesn't want that."

"Whyever not?" I asked, grimacing as Red Daniel gave a mighty tug on his rope, shifting the load and almost burying Little Daniel under the bureau.

"You don't know his girls!" said Jake, laughing.

When Red Daniel and Little Daniel finally departed, Jake and I set out to find Elam, who had ridden over earlier with our crusty neighbor, Nate Stoltzfus. We found the two examining a flatbed wagon.

The old man nodded frostily in our direction. "Chake," he said, pronouncing Jake's name with the Dutch *ch*. He nodded briefly to me, eyed my jeans, scarlet shirt, and wildly patterned sweater with a jaundiced eye, then left immediately, his old back straight and proud.

"About one-quarter of the Amish are named Stoltzfus," Jake said as he watched the old man go. "It means 'proud foot.' My father says it means the Stoltzfuses have their feet planted firmly and proudly on the faith. I don't know. It seems too kind an explanation for some people."

Elam grinned at his brother. "Nasty, nasty, Chake. You know what Mom'd say if she heard you."

The brothers looked at each other and began chanting in unison, "'Let no corrupt communication proceed out of your mouth, but that which is good for the use of edifying, that it may minister grace to the hearers.'" Only they said it in High German, not King James English.

After Elam translated for me, Jake said, "Whenever we kids got mad at each other and started yelling, Mom ran that by us."

"And, himmel," said Elam. "If we ever said anything against another in the community, we had to repeat the verse and ask for forgiveness from God."

"Mom ran a tough shop," said Jake with admiration. "Great lady."

Elam shrugged, uncomfortable with the compliment. "She was chust doing what was right. Now where'd you hide the van? I've got the tools Father wanted and for less than he felt was an acceptable price."

"Good going," Jake said. "He'll like that. No man appreciates a bargain more than Father."

Wondering how two such different men could come from the same home and training, I watched the brothers put what looked like a collection of rusty antiques into the back of the van.

"What will you do with them?" I asked.

"Make our own repairs on bridles and other equipment," Elam said. "We have a little blacksmith shop set up in the shed beside the barn. It's hard to get things repaired these days, especially the hardware on the buggies. It's a dying art, so we do as much of our own repair work as possible."

"What about the guys who made the buggies originally? Won't they do the repairs for you? Sort of like a car dealership?"

Elam shook his head. "There are too few of them, not nearly enough to meet the demand. We ordered a new buggy months ago. I doubt we'll get it before winter."

Elam turned to Jake. "By the way, Nate told me that he's noticed a car hanging around our farm recently."

"How in the world did he notice a car around our farm?" Then Jake grinned broadly as a thought popped into his mind. "Binoculars? He spies on us? Isn't there a law against that somewhere in the Ordnung? There must be!"

Elam smiled and shook his head hopelessly at his brother's glee. "I didn't ask how he knew. I chust thanked him for the information. He said the car often parks on the wagon road that cuts between our two farms, and it always faces us. Father and I have been working on the other side of the farm baling hay, so I've never seen it."

"Neither have I," Jake said as he looked thoughtfully at me. "But I'll certainly be watching from now on."

I was willing to bet that the driver wore a Braves cap.

When we arrived home, I carried my painting and supplies inside and hurried to get ready before Clarke came for me. I had been so pleased when he actually called and asked me to save the evening for him that I'd sputtered. I'm sure I did.

At one point in my preparations I glanced at myself in the mirror and was surprised by my sparkling eyes and high color. I shook my head in despair. I was so transparent!

"What am I going to do with you, woman?" I grinned at myself, then stared in disbelief at my cheek.

Where Hawk had gotten me with his fang, I now had a little scar that made a perfect dimple! I smiled again to make certain, and *voila!* There it was again.

I'd always wanted a dimple. When I was growing up, I had a blonde friend named Marly who was so subtle and understated that I always felt as though I had a megaphone in my hand and a laugh track in my voice box. She floated when she walked, and she wore soft yellows and creams and baby blue. And she had a dimple in each cheek. All the boys swarmed to her, and when she favored one with a smile, the dimples knocked them mute.

And now I had a dimple too! I no longer wanted to be a powder blue blonde—too anemic—but I loved my new dimple. When Clarke showed up, I was careful to smile as broadly as I could. I did not knock him mute.

"How'd you like to see Adam Hurlbert in action?" he asked as we walked to his car.

"You're taking me to a thousand-dollar-a-plate dinner! How nice! I'm so glad I'm wearing my best jeans and plaid blazer."

Clarke grinned at me. What a gorgeous smile. "He's speaking at a rally at Park City Mall at six. We could listen to him, then go get dinner."

"Happy days are here again," I sang. "Sounds good to me."

We found a large crowd gathered at one end of the parking lot at Park City and joined them.

"Shall we push our way to the front?" Clarke asked.

I looked at the wall of backs we'd have to work our way

through and shook my head. "I think I like it right here."

A raised platform jaunty in red, white, and blue bunting, waited for Adam and Irene.

It wasn't too long before a helicopter appeared overhead and lowered itself to the ground amid a great rush of wind and gravel. Obviously Adam and his campaign people had a handle on the effect of that cornerstone of good theater, the entrance.

"Only fifteen minutes late," said Clarke. "Not bad."

"Whetting our appetites," I agreed.

The door of the helicopter opened, and Adam and Irene stepped out, flanked by advisors and security and followed by the detestable Nelson.

The lead people cut a path through the crowd, much as Moses split the Red Sea. People fell back willingly, standing on tiptoe to catch a glimpse of the celebrities. Cheers of "Yea, Adam!" and "Hurlbert for president!" rang above the high-school band that played "America the Beautiful."

"Hurlbert for president?" I said.

"A partisan who plans ahead," Clarke replied.

He reached out to rest a hand on my shoulder just as a very round, very enthusiastic lady pushed between us and stopped there. I looked over her head at Clarke, who shrugged helplessly.

The woman held a handmade sign painted on a yellow pillowcase, waving it vigorously over her head. I had to duck to avoid getting it flung into the side of my head. *Hurlbert today to save the USA,* it read.

Suddenly she planted herself firmly about two inches in front of me, put her fingers between her teeth, and gave the loudest, shrillest whistle I'd ever heard. All the people nearby shook their heads and looked dazed. I was sure I was permanently deafened.

I couldn't help but laugh as I watched Clarke, glassy eyed,

give an abrupt head shake to clear his unexpected case of tinnitus. The din in my own head gradually lessened, just in time for the next verbal onslaught.

"Come here, Barney!" the woman screamed at a decibel level OSHA would declare requires ear protection for anyone within five miles. She reached through the crowd to a little old man who wore a scowl of heroic proportions and a parka three sizes too big. I got the distinct impression that he wished he were anywhere but here, especially when she plucked him bodily to stand beside her, further separating me from Clarke.

"Hold this, Barney," she ordered, thrusting one corner of the pillowcase into his hand. "Now wave it!" She lifted her hand high and began vigorously fluttering the pillowcase. "I want him to see us. I want to be on TV with him. I want the newspeople to talk with us so we can tell everyone how wonderful he is. Now wave! Like you mean it!"

The little man dutifully raised his arm and began to move the sign back and forth, back and forth, but not like he meant it. The end result of their partnership was that the lady turned red from the exertion, the man kept dropping his end of the pillowcase as her vigor pulled it out of his hand, and the message was totally unreadable.

I was trying to stifle an impolite laugh when I was abruptly and savagely pushed from behind. I shot forward, literally lifted off my feet, but I could do nothing to save myself because of the press of the crowd. I let out a long "Ohhhh!" as I collided violently with the chubby whistler-sign waver. We fell to the ground in a great and unladylike tangle of arms and legs.

"I'm sorry! I'm sorry!" I kept repeating as totally unsuitable giggles escaped. I had this vision of what we looked like as we thrashed about trying to get up, and every time I saw it in my mind, fresh giggles slipped out.

Kind hands reached out and pulled the two of us to our feet. Clarke held me up with a strong arm about my waist.

"Are you okay?" he asked.

I looked at him and giggled. I slapped my hand over my mouth. When I thought I could talk without embarrassing myself further, I said, "I think so."

I had a hole in my jeans and a skinned knee. My sore hip had taken another shot, but otherwise I was fine. I giggled anew at the sight of *Hurlbert today to save the USA* draped over Barney's thin shoulders.

"Oh, Bitsy! Oh, Bitsy!" He was genuinely distressed. "Oh, Bitsy, are you all right?"

My unwilling human cushion had a bloody nose and badly scraped hands. As soon as I saw the blood streaming down her front, I sobered abruptly.

"I'm sorry," I said again, this time with great sincerity. "He pushed me and I lost my bal—"

I stopped and looked frantically around, already knowing what had happened.

"My purse! Clarke! My purse has been stolen!"

"What?"

I groaned. "My purse! My credit cards. My license. My checkbook. My new phone! This time it's really gone!"

Clarke looked around as if he expected the thief to be standing next to us waiting to be spotted.

"Did you see a man in a Braves cap?" I asked him.

"A baseball cap?"

"A Braves cap," I repeated. "Did anyone see a man in a Braves cap?" I looked around the circle of people who had collected about us. Of course, no one had.

A police officer arrived about then to check out the disturbance. She escorted Clarke and me and Bitsy and Barney to an area inside the mall that was obviously the control center for the political appearance. Bitsy mumbled through the yellow pillowcase pressed to her nose that she was Mrs. Bitsy Snodgrass and the little man was her husband, Barney Snodgrass.

"We just love Adam Hurlbert," she said as she pulled the pillowcase away to check if the blood was still flowing. It was. She reapplied it. "Seeing him like this—it's the high point of our lives."

Barney looked skeptical.

As a nurse tended to Bitsy, the officer talked with me.

"I'm sorry, Miss Matthews," she said. "Unfortunately such petty crimes are commonplace at large gatherings like rallies and concerts."

"It's the second time it's happened," I said forlornly, my mind still on all the things I'd need to replace.

"The second time?"

"Well, not quite the second time. Someone tried to get my purse the other night, but he wasn't successful." I felt very tired.

"Are you having trouble with someone specific bothering you?" she asked with great interest.

I thought of the Braves cap, but I didn't know that he had anything to do with this evening or with the attempt at the hospital. Besides, "Look for a man in a Braves cap" wouldn't be terribly helpful. I shook my head. "It must be coincidence."

She nodded, disappointed, and finished filling out the police report.

"We'll contact you if we recover your property," she assured me. I nodded without any hope.

Just then Adam and Irene Hurlbert were ushered into the room. Adam was deep in conversation with a tall, bony, anorexic-looking young man while Irene, oozing charm and graciousness, was talking to a woman who was obviously a reporter. I watched, interested in seeing these two up close and in action. Irene was beautiful, no doubt about it, and Adam was every bit as handsome as I'd thought that day in the hospital corridor. And he definitely treated his hair.

Another man walked up to Adam and his companion and talked quietly for a couple of minutes. As he talked, the politician looked at me and Bitsy. I smiled, flashing my new dimple, and Bitsy simpered in spite of the cotton packing her right nostril. Shaking his head as if greatly distressed, Adam walked over to us.

"My dear lady!" He took Bitsy's hand in his, patted it gently, and kept it. "To have been injured at a rally sponsored by my people! Please accept my sincerest apologies and make sure we receive any medical bills that might result from this monstrous occurrence. We must make this terrible thing right and restore your confidence in Lancaster County. You may be certain that if I'm elected, things like this will not continue to happen here in the Commonwealth of Pennsylvania."

I glanced at Clarke to see his response to this gushing performance and watched one of those fascinating dark eyebrows arch in skepticism over that campaign promise. We—and certainly Adam—knew it had as much chance of being fulfilled as I had of being hung in the Philadelphia Museum of Art.

But Adam knew how to read his future constituents. Bitsy seemed willing to buy the whole utopian idea. In fact, the blitzed Bitsy seemed willing to buy any idea the man had to offer. With a final pat on the hand he had held throughout their entire conversation, he turned to me.

"And you, young lady," he said, adopting a brisk, businesslike tone. He took my hand, pressed it briefly, then dropped it. "I understand you had the misfortune of being robbed this evening. Please accept my apologies that such a thing happened at one of our rallies. Let my office expedite the replacement of your license and any other items within our purview."

"Thank you for your concern and for your help. I appreciate them both," I said politely. My mom would have been proud.

"It's the least we can do," he said sincerely, reaching to shake Clarke's hand too. "And you, sir, take good care of her." The handshake he offered Clarke was firm, quick, and manly. I was willing to bet that Adam Hurlbert's handlers had discussed exactly what was the acceptable flesh-pressing time for different types of voters. He'd learned the lessons well.

As Adam Hurlbert smiled charmingly at me one more time, I had to admit it: the guy was really, really good. I just hoped I hadn't looked as delighted as I felt when he'd taken my hand in his and given it that quick, warm squeeze. At least I hadn't drooled like Bitsy.

A tug on my arm turned my attention from the smooth politician. Standing before me was Nelson, curiosity bristling from every inch of his lumpy little body. I had forgotten all about him.

"What happened, Miss Matthews?" He was all agog as he took in my torn jeans and bleeding knee and Bitsy's wounds and bloody pillowcase.

"She was robbed, Son," said Adam pontifically. "Isn't that terrible?"

"Yeah?" Nelson's eyes nearly popped out of his head. "Wow! I didn't know people robbed teachers. Wait till the guys at school hear!"

I hoped my lip wasn't curled in a snarl when I said,

"Thanks for the sympathy, Nelson."

The kid was in his glory. Not only a helicopter ride, but crime and blood and guts.

"What happened to the fat lady?" He pointed indelicately at Bitsy.

"I bumped into her."

Nelson laughed happily. "Hey, Mom!" he screamed across the room. "My art teacher beat up on this fat lady!"

Irene's flawless eyebrows arched delicately as she looked at me. "Really?"

"Shh, Nelson," said Adam. He grabbed for the boy's shoulder and missed as Nelson skillfully dodged. "We must let these kind people go. They've had a very tiring night."

Nelson, however, stepped closer, planting himself in front of Clarke.

"Are you Miss Matthews's boyfriend?" he asked in a typical display of tact.

Clarke nodded. "And may you be so lucky when you grow up."

Nelson blinked and looked at me, clearly seeing me in a whole new light. "Wow!" he said.

My thought exactly.

FOURTEEN

There was a great surge of activity around the farm, movement I was aware of without consciously realizing it.

Jake was suddenly engrossed in painting the porch railing and fence that lined the yard, using a special long-handled brush that Elam had made for him. Elam was on a ladder painting windows. Ruth had taken time from her pretzel factory again, and every time I saw her, she was in the kitchen with her mother, busy about the stove. Mary had stopped going to the farmers' market and was seeing that all the preserves, apple butter, and chips got stored in the basement. One day I came home from school to find the entire family cleaning and whitewashing the cellar, which had already been scrupulously clean.

The reason for all this activity became obvious the last Sunday in October, two weeks after Elam and Ruth knelt to take the vows of their church. It was a messy, cold, rainy day, the nasty kind of autumn day that made me wonder if Todd hadn't been right about my freezing this winter. My little ceramic heater was chugging away, and heat rose through a grate in the hall by the stairs—but it wasn't central heating.

I wrapped myself in several layers of clothes as quickly as I could and hurried downstairs to enjoy the radiant warmth coming from the great wood stove. I planned to sit beside it and warm my outsides while I drank a huge cup of tea to warm my insides.

"Ruth!" I stopped and stared at the girl sitting in the rocker by the window, reading. I had never seen her read before. But the bigger cause for surprise was that I had heard the Zooks leave for church hours ago. I distinctly remembered thinking how uncomfortable a buggy must be on a day like this and how thankful I was for the heater in my yellow car.

"What are you doing here?" I asked. "Don't you feel well?"

Ruth grinned. "I feel great! In fact, I've rarely felt better."

There was an undercurrent of excitement crackling about the girl. Her gray eyes sparkled, her color was high, and she seemed more like the ever active Elam than her usual quiet self.

"What's going on?" I demanded.

"She and Isaiah are being published today," said Jake from the doorway of his apartment. "That means the minister's announcing their engagement."

So Jake had anticipated correctly. I hugged the girl. "I'm so happy for you! Now all I need to do is meet your Isaiah."

"You will," said Ruth. "And very soon. He'll be living here from now until the wedding."

I blinked. "Here? Really? And when is the wedding?"

"A week from Thursday."

"You're getting married—" I counted quickly—"eleven days from now?"

Ruth nodded happily. "The first Thursday in November, the first good date we could pick."

"There'll be weddings every Tuesday and Thursday in November and into December," Jake explained. "Sometimes there'll be more than one a day. Harvesting's done, and it's time to relax before preparing everything for next year. It's the one time all year that weddings won't interfere with farming. There's plenty of time for visiting and celebrating."

"But how will you ever get everything ready so fast?" I

asked. I felt overwhelmed, and it wasn't even my wedding.

"Oh, most things are ready already. We—or I should say Isaiah—have to ask the people we want to help with the wedding meal and the couples we'd like to be in the wedding, but much of the other preparation is done. Why do you think we've been painting and cleaning like crazy? And why do you think Mom and I have been baking and storing so much food?"

"Then you've quit your pretzel job for good?"

She nodded. "There's no need for me to work anymore. Besides, there isn't time. There's still a lot to do to get ready. And then afterwards we'll be visiting relatives for a while."

"Where will you live when you've finished visiting?" I asked, thinking that I'd like a more private honeymoon when it was my turn. People in the next room listening to creaky beds wasn't my idea of how to begin a marriage.

"Besides their family farm, Isaiah's father has a small farm in Honey Brook, not too far from where my sister Sarah and Abner live. We'll live there."

"How very nice for you," I said, meaning every word. "With land being so scarce, you're very lucky to have your own place."

"I don't think Isaiah could be happy if he wasn't farming," Ruth said. "He loves it. And I'm going to love being his wife." She grinned at me with the delightful smugness of someone who's getting exactly what she wants.

I thought about Ruth's impending marriage all the way to church. I found it fascinating to think about how settled the girl was, how secure she felt in her thinking, how lacking in curiosity she was about life beyond Isaiah and the Amish community. She would marry, have children, live and die in the same pattern as generations of Amish women before her. She wouldn't be moved to go back to school at forty-five as my mother had been. In fact, should such a thought enter her mind, she would squelch it. Education made you proud and interfered with the development of that much desired quality, humility.

Did Ruth ever feel shortchanged by her life? I didn't think so. In a culture that gave few choices, she appeared satisfied with what I saw as limited and limiting horizons.

Even her quiet rebellion had not been so much against Amish legalisms as against biblical standards. When she and Isaiah went off on their jaunts, they were still readily identifiable as Amish. Kapp, straight pins and black stockings, black brimmed hat, broadfall trousers and suspenders—all were in place. It was not the Ordnung that got short shrift in Ruth's life; it was the Word of God.

Not that Ruth's life was bad by any means. Just the opposite. She was part of a close, loving, encouraging family and community. Many English would give all they had to belong like that. Ruth knew Isaiah wouldn't leave her. She knew she'd always have a home, always have someone to look after her, always know exactly what was expected of her.

I shook my head as I pulled into the parking lot at church. Not for me such well-ordered rigidity. The exhilarating freedom of being a Christian woman with a future limited only by the will of God was something I'd never change for temporal security. I liked asking questions, trying new things, exploring my options. I was a modern Christian, not one caught in a pleasant and loving time warp. God and I—together we would make the many choices in my life.

Though, Lord, it would be wonderful if Clarke were part of it. What do you think?

~~~~~

It wasn't until after church that it dawned on me that the Zooks should be allowed to celebrate Ruth's engagement without an interloper hanging over their shoulders. But what would I do if I didn't go home? Clarke was away today, speaking at a friend's church, and doing anything with Todd was out of the question. I thought for a minute and decided to drive over to Honey Brook where Ruth and Isaiah would be living. Not that I expected to find their exact farm, but I could see the area.

I took Route 23 east to Route 10. There I stopped at the Windmill Family Restaurant for a quick lunch, then I drove south on Route 10. When I got close to Honey Brook, I began taking side roads. I thought once again how beautiful this whole area was, whether back in Lancaster County or just across the line into Chester County where I now was. I loved the patchwork-quilt farms and rolling vistas, the wandering streams, and the rich black soil. Even with the end of the color and richness of the growing season, the countryside filled my artist's eye with light and shadow, harmony and contrast.

Everywhere I drove, I saw signs of the growing cottage industries among the Amish—greenhouses, woodworking shops, signs announcing the selling of quilts, preserves and baked goods, picnic benches, puppies and rabbits. All the signs also read CLOSED SUNDAYS. These businesses were the practical way the Amish dealt with the twin concerns of dwindling farmland and increasing population. I was struck again with what a marvelous mixture of accommodation and isolation the Amish were.

Eventually I came to the steep hills south of Honey Brook where Jake had his accident. I looked again at the side of the road for the cross marking that intersection as a death spot. I wanted to stop and examine the cross, to see if there was a name written on it, to wonder what had happened to this person.

But with a long line of traffic behind me, I couldn't stop, but had to drive through the intersection. I came almost immediately to a business drive on the left. I pulled in and turned the wheel, stopping just before I drove back onto the road. I looked the area over carefully, and my eye was drawn to the house nearest the intersection. Maybe those people knew something about the accident the cross commemorated. Maybe they knew something about Jake's, too.

I noted the name on the mailbox as I pulled up to the house: Martin. A good Lancaster County name relocated here in Chester County.

I rang the bell, and a woman about my mother's age answered. I introduced myself.

"I'm interested in information about the cross at the intersection. Do you know anything about it?"

"I should say I do," the woman said. "My daughter Rose put it up and takes care of it. Come on in and you can talk to her."

Mrs. Martin led me to her living room and left me in a navy overstuffed chair with a Wedgwood-blue and rose afghan lying over its back. She was back in a moment with a young woman with curly brown hair and glasses over brown eyes.

"I'm Rose," she said. "Mom says you want to know about the cross."

I nodded. "I have a friend who was hurt at this intersection too, so I was wondering what your story is."

Rose walked to the bow window and looked out across the lawn to the cross.

"I'm a nurse," she said. "I should have been able to save him."

Her voice and face were full of pain.

"When did it happen?" I asked.

"Last October. October 20 to be exact. The worst day of my life. My fiancé and I had a horrible fight. I broke up with him and he got furious, even nasty. I'd never seen him like that before." She shook her head at the memory.

"When I handed him his ring, he rushed outside into the rain, ran across the yard, and threw the ring into the field across the street. He yelled, 'If you don't wear this, no one wears it!'"

"He threw away a diamond ring?" I was incredulous.

"A bit melodramatic, wouldn't you say?" Rose put her hand to her forehead and rubbed.

"A bit idiotic, I'd say," said Mrs. Martin.

"Mom," said Rose with gentle warning.

Mrs. Martin ignored Rose and turned to me. "We never did like him," she said. "We thought he was two-faced, a hypocrite. But Rose couldn't see it."

"I couldn't," Rose agreed.

"We thank God every day that she broke up with him."

"Are you sure he didn't just fake throwing the ring to make you feel worse?" I asked.

"I've thought of that, especially since Mom and I have searched for the thing over and over all year with no luck." She shrugged. "I really don't care."

"I do," said Mrs. Martin. "I want to get some value out of the mess he made!"

Rose shook her head. "Mom, not now. Kristie doesn't want to hear your opinion of Ben."

"She already did," said Mrs. Martin. She put her hand up quickly to silence Rose who was getting agitated. "I know, I've said too much already." She got to her feet. "I'll try to redeem myself by leaving you two alone."

Rose watched her mother leave the room. "She's still mad at him for all that he put me through."

I nodded, thinking of Mary's pain over Jake. "Moms are like that."

Rose went on with her story. "After he threw the ring and yelled a few other lovely things at me, Ben got into his car and roared out of the drive. I turned to go back inside the house, trying to decide whether I was relieved or devastated. That's when I heard a screech of metal. I turned and saw sparks sliding along the road, then I heard a thud and a terrible scream. There are no streetlights out here, and the night was dark because of the clouds. I ran to see what had happened, and there was a man pinned under a motorcycle."

"A man under a motorcycle?" Wait a minute!

She nodded and shivered. "I knelt beside him and felt for his pulse. I had to leave him to rush back and call for the ambulance. Then I went back and sat with him until the ambulance and the medic unit from the trauma center over at Brandywine Hospital in Coatesville came. They ended up med-evacing him. They put the helicopter down in the field over there." She pointed directly across the road from her house.

In my mind I could see the flashing lights, hear the crackle of static from car radios, feel the cold wash of the rain, smell the leaking gasoline, sense the fear. And I could see Rose sitting by the road, holding the hand of the injured man, talking, talking to help fight shock, both his and hers.

"I sat in the rain with him for twenty minutes or more," she said. "He was in and out of consciousness, but he didn't seem to be in pain, which worried me a lot. As the medics worked on him, I saw them look at each other and shake their heads. No hope. No hope. That's how I knew he was going to die. 'Hold on!' I yelled at him as they carried him to the helicopter.

But he was unconscious. Then suddenly the helicopter was gone, and so were the emergency vehicles. It was just us Martins again, and we never heard another word about anything. But I made him the cross."

"Oh, Rose!" I was so excited I was bouncing. "I don't think he died. I think that was my friend Jake."

"What?"

"It was Jake! It had to be Jake. How many motorcycle accidents have you had out here? He's a paraplegic, but he's very much alive!"

Her hands clutched each other in her lap, and her face was tense. "How can I find out if it's really him?"

"I know Jake's accident was last October, but I don't remember the date. And I know it was at this intersection. I'll talk to him and then call you."

"Could you call him now?" she asked.

"No," I said. "I think it deserves a face-to-face conversation because the accident is such a painful subject for him. But I'll talk to him a soon as I can and let you know."

Rose stared at me, tears in her eyes. "I've always thought the accident happened because Ben ran the stop sign when he left here in such a temper. I don't know that, because I didn't see it, but he lives in that direction. I've always blamed myself. If it weren't for me, Ben wouldn't have been mad. If it weren't for me, he wouldn't have run that sign. If it weren't for me, that man wouldn't have died. It would be such a relief if he weren't dead after all!"

I bet it would, after living with all that guilt for a year.

And, of course, he wasn't dead. He was alive and grumpy right up in Bird-in-Hand. Rose cried when I called her and told her that her cross could be taken down. No one had died that evening at that intersection, though I wasn't convinced that he was completely living yet either. But time and God could deal with that.

"You ought to meet her, Jake," I said to him one evening. "She's a very nice person and she's cute, too. I think she'd feel so much better seeing you."

"Did she suggest this meeting?" he asked in an icy voice.

"No. It's my idea. You look good and are doing so well with your driving and all. It would set her mind at rest."

"Absolutely not!" he said, surprising me. "I do not want to meet this woman."

"She sat with you in the rain," I said, trying to shame him into it. "She made a cross in your honor."

"Kristie, don't push me. I do not want to meet her! Let me have some dignity, would you?" And he stormed off to his rooms.

I sat in the front room and tried to understand why he was so angry with what I still thought was a great idea. The closest I could figure was that he was embarrassed that Rose had seen him as he'd been that night, injured, diminished, and in a situation totally beyond his control.

That was when I realized that Jake, for all his passivity, was a control freak. In fact, I now understood, his passivity was his control mechanism for a life that was largely beyond him right now.

Poor Jake.

The Sunday after Ruth and Isaiah's banns were published proved to be another rainy, cold day. As I drove to church, I hoped Thursday would be better for the wedding. After all the cleaning around the farm, it would be a shame if the mud and mess of a rainy day dimmed the gleam and shine of everyone's hard work. And where would they put well over a hundred people if some couldn't stand around talking outside while others sat eating inside? The barn?

I spent the morning in kindergarten church due to an emergency call the night before from the November lady, who had a sick child. I was more than willing to help her out. Some of the children were squirmier than usual, but attendance was low, probably due to the weather. Or maybe they all had the same thing the November lady's son had.

My paper-bag pumpkins were a big success, though some of the drawn-on faces required loving parental imagination to discern the features. But the kids were proud of their work, and that was what counted.

I waved good-bye to my last charge and gathered my supplies. With luck—You're a Christian, Matthews, you don't believe in luck—I'd see Clarke, and we could go get something to eat. I could tell him Rose's story. Maybe we could talk about Ruth's wedding. With his knowledge of the Plain culture, he could probably tell me what to expect as far as the actual wedding ceremony itself.

I smiled to myself. One topic was as good as another. It was the man across the table who was important.

I smiled as I thought about Clarke. I hadn't seen him since the Hurlbert rally, and I missed him. I couldn't deny it. I didn't even know him that well yet, and already I felt closer to him that I ever had to Todd. When we were together, it seemed he felt the same way. But he hadn't called. I kept telling myself that was because he taught and counseled at night and I taught during the day.

I was belting my raincoat, humming to myself about being

in love with a wonderful guy, when I glanced out the window. There was Clarke hurrying to his car. Without waiting to see me. And he wasn't alone.

He had his arm around the waist of a slim young woman who was trying to hold her umbrella over the two of them with somewhat limited success. Clarke was laughing as the rain slid off the umbrella and down his collar.

How noble that he can laugh, I thought with sudden venom.

I was both surprised and appalled at the ferocity of my thoughts. For all I knew, Clarke was merely helping someone to her car. He was, after all, a nice guy and a gentleman.

Yeah, right. I watched with a sinking heart and thought of the times he had put his arm around my waist.

Clarke and the woman reached his car, where he opened the passenger door and assisted her in. He and she laughed together as she attempted to get the umbrella down and in without getting all wet.

Cute, I thought sourly. So cute.

Clarke climbed in his side of the car, and the girl turned to him. She threw her arms around him and kissed him happily on the cheek. Then she reached out and rubbed the side of his face, probably removing lipstick. He reached over and ruffled her hair. They drove away without a backward glance.

Waves of depression washed over me. I had thought—as recently as five minutes ago—that I was in the beginning stages of a most promising romance. Apparently I was the only one who thought so. I had leaped to a conclusion because the man had looked at me kindly a few times and indicated to Nelson that he was my boyfriend—though now that I thought about it, he had never actually said those words. Nelson had.

Clarke'd just been too polite to embarrass me in front of the obnoxious child.

I obviously was misinterpreting his intentions to fit my wishes. A dinner with his aunt and uncle, two hospital taxi runs, a purse snatching, and a ride on a railroad do not make a deathless romance. In reality they don't even make a good friendship.

Let's put things in perspective, Matthews, shall we?

I walked slowly to my car, strangely satisfied that the skies were crying with me. I couldn't help wondering if Ruth's ordered life allowed for romantic misjudgments like mine. Had she and Isaiah ever had a misunderstanding of any significance?

Or was I just experiencing the "freedom" I'd been so superior about?

I began to sing.

"Alas, my love, you do me wrong
To cast me off discourteously…"

FIFTEEN

When I climbed into my car, I just sat behind the wheel, staring at the empty parking lot without seeing it. I was more than a little surprised at the intensity of the despair that twisted my heart. I knew I cared a lot for Clarke, but there was no doubt that I had fallen a lot harder than I realized. Even the simple act of breathing had become difficult.

I watched the rivulets of water slide down the windshield and thought melodramatically that I was watching my life slide away too, quietly, colorlessly, inevitably, disappearing into the gloom.

I remembered his hand cupping my cheek, his arm about my shoulders, his "You should be so lucky" to the lumpy Nelson. He bought one of my paintings, for Pete's sake! I sighed from the soles of my feet and wearily turned the key.

When the engine of my sunshine-yellow car turned over as usual, I was strangely offended.

"Don't you realize that we're broken here?" I asked. My voice caught on the word *broken*.

The car's mechanical heart didn't understand, and the purring continued. I drove to a McDonald's drive-thru, where I ordered a cheeseburger and a Coke. When they handed me the food, the smell made me nauseated. I handed it back to the disbelieving boy and drove away without even asking for my money back.

Still enveloped in the melancholy that had made it impossible for me to deal with my lunch, I drove to Holiday House and made my way to Mr. Geohagan's room. I paused inside his door, seeing Clarke huddled cozily under an umbrella, seeing him receive a kiss on the cheek as clearly as if he and the blonde were there in the room with me. I blinked against the tears.

It took me a minute to realize that Mr. Geohagan was every bit as preoccupied as I was, but that's where the similarity ended. Where I was drained, weary, and hurt, he was alert, involved, and all but sitting at attention as he listened intently to a man standing beside his bed. The stranger spoke to Mr. Geohagan in clipped, forceful sentences, and I was struck by the visual contrast between the frail old man in the bed and the tall, extremely thin visitor who exuded energy.

"I'm sure you understand our concern," the man said.

Mr. Geohagan nodded. "Oh, I understand the problem quite clearly. But as far as I'm concerned, you needn't worry. Remember that something like this can affect me every bit as much as the rest of you."

"That's what I keep telling everyone, and I almost believe myself." The man rubbed his fingers back and forth across his forehead as if it hurt. "You're as involved as the rest of us, more if the truth be known. You wouldn't do anything to upset things. You couldn't. But you understand why I have to ask."

"Sure," Mr. Geohagan said. "Don't worry. You can trust me, Bill."

The men's eyes locked with unusual intensity, and I felt waves of hidden meaning roll over the room like hurricane surf.

"If you say I needn't worry, Ev, I won't," the visitor said, but I heard reserve and uncertainty in his tone. "Your word has always been trustworthy."

"And it still is."

"There's a lot at stake here. A lot."

"I know exactly what's at stake," Mr. Geohagan said, his voice every bit as clipped and urgent as his visitor's. "And as you said, I have every bit as much riding on this whole thing as you do."

The man looked out the window. "Quite honestly, Ev, we're worried about you."

Mr. Geohagan smiled sourly. "You're so thoughtful to be concerned about my health."

"That's not—" the man began, then turned abruptly and strode from the room, his face angry and uncertain. He was no more aware of me than Mr. Geohagan was.

That's okay, guys, I thought. I feel pretty invisible anyway. Unnoticed. Unappreciated. Unwanted.

My mother, a very practical and commonsense lady, always got angry at me when the melancholy part of my personality kicked in.

"I don't care if artists are emotional," she'd say, finger waving in a most choleric way under my nose. "That's no excuse for letting your feelings run away with you. You always assume the worst. You always know it's the end of the world." She'd make an unpleasant noise in the back of her throat. "Kristie, for heaven's sake, get some backbone!"

Well, Mom, maybe tomorrow. Maybe it won't hurt as much then.

But I suspected it would. Tomorrow and tomorrow and tomorrow.

When the tall man strode from the room, Mr. Geohagan fell back on his pillows, completely spent, his eyes closed, his breathing raspy and strained. He scared me enough to pull me out of my morose and myopic self-absorption. Suddenly my pain wasn't the most important thing.

"Are you all right? What can I get for you?" I asked, hurrying forward. "Tell me what I should do."

Mr. Geohagan's eyes flew open, and I saw fear there, and desperation.

"My oxygen," he whispered.

I pushed the buzzer beside his bed and held his hand as we waited for the nurse to come. Holiday House had, so far, been more than I had expected. The care was excellent.

"You mustn't allow that man to upset you," I said. "It sounded to me like he was trying to bully you."

"Don't worry about it," he rasped, pausing to breathe after every two or three words. "I upset him more than he upsets me." His lips twisted in what was supposed to be a sly smile. "And I love it."

"Mr. Geohagan! I'm surprised at you!" I said it lightly, as though he had made a joke.

"I can be a pretty tough old guy if I need to be."

His thin hand went to his chest, and his whole body heaved as he struggled to draw in the air to sustain himself. I found myself taking great sympathetic gulps of air. I felt the way I had that day in the ER when I was certain he would die before Harriet returned. This time he was going to die before the nurse came. I pressed the emergency button several more times.

"Kristie, will you do me a favor?" His hand grasped mine with unexpected strength, though his voice was barely audible.

"Shh, don't get agitated." I patted his shoulder. "Of course I will." I imagined the terror of gasping, of having lungs so impaired that they no longer could expand and contract enough to provide the necessary oxygen to my body.

"I need some things from storage."

"What do you need, and where are they stored?"

"A garage. The key." He gestured toward the bedside table. "In the top drawer."

I opened the drawer and took out the key, its mystery now solved. A storage garage, of all things.

A nurse suddenly appeared, and I backed out of the way. In a few seconds the cannula for the oxygen was in place under Mr. Geohagan's nose, and in a few minutes he was breathing much more easily. While he rested for a bit, I sat and read the Sunday news—or tried to. My powers of concentration weren't working very well.

"Much better now," he said after about ten minutes, then returned immediately to the subject on his mind. "Now this garage. I rented it so I'd have someplace to keep the things Doris and I had. When I sold our house, I just couldn't bring myself to throw my whole life away. I felt dead enough as it was. So I stored it all."

I thought of Emily Dickinson.

The bustle in the house
The morning after death
Is solemnest of industries
Enacted upon earth,—

The sweeping up the heart,
And putting love away
We shall not want to use again
Until eternity.

I hoped he thought my sudden sniffling was allergies.

"Bring me everything on the desk," he whispered. "And everything in the left-hand file drawer."

I listened carefully as Mr. Geohagan described the garage's location.

We both fell silent, he to rest, I to feign reading. When I looked up some time later, I found him studying me.

"What's the matter with you?" he asked. His voice, though far from strong, was much firmer.

"Nothing."

"Ha! Don't give me that. Hasn't anyone ever told you you're a bad liar?"

"As a matter of fact, yes."

He nodded. "So what's his name?"

"What?"

"What's his name? A hound-dog face like yours usually means some man's been doing some dirty work."

"How'd you get to be so smart?" I asked.

"Cathleen," he said. "I learned a lot of painful lessons from her near the end."

I nodded. I just bet he did. I was silent a minute, thinking of her extreme response to a failed romance. I knew that no matter how much I hurt, I would always consider that way no way.

"I don't know that anyone's actually been unkind to me," I finally said. "It just seems that all the castles and happily-ever-afters were in my imagination. I read more into things than was there." I shrugged. "It happens all the time, though not usually to me."

"Well, any man who'd let you get away must be crazy."

I smiled at him. "You are very gallant, sir. And while I agree with your assessment of things, I'm still stuck with having to resort to the old stiff upper lip and lots of prayer."

"I doubt either will do you any good," he pronounced. "What you need is another object for your affections."

Right. At the snap of my fingers. "I can tell you haven't tried to date recently. Nice guys are scarcer than hen's teeth."

"No nice guys at work? Or where you live?"

"All the men where I work are already spoken for, and I live on an Amish farm, remember? I don't think I'd be happy married to an Amishman no matter how nice he was. Culture and stuff."

"They're religious like you."

"They're religious, but not like me. Not like me at all. It's works versus grace."

"Whatever. Where'd you meet your last beau?"

I giggled. "Beau? You're revealing your age. And I met him at the farm. He's the one whose car I bled all over the day I got bitten."

"And you don't want to resort to another physical ploy to get a new man? If it worked once…"

"This face can only take so many risks." I felt my dimple-scar. "There has to be a better way, because I might not be so lucky next time."

"Don't you have a favorite bar where some decent guys hang out?"

"I'm afraid I'm more a church mouse than a bar maid."

"Did this man go to church?"

I nodded. "It was one of the many things I liked about him."

"You can't trust men who go to church, Kristie."

"What?"

"I mean it. They're too honestly stupid."

I blinked, missing his strange logic.

Mr. Geohagan nodded. "They don't lie on their income taxes. They don't cheat on their wives. They don't speed. No, cut that one. Maybe they do. But they don't take money out of the collection plate. And they don't know right from wrong."

I laughed. "Don't you think you're being a bit inconsistent? It sounds to me like you've listed some very desirable traits, except for the last one."

He shrugged. "Maybe."

"Okay, I'll bite. Why don't men who go to church know right from wrong?"

"Because they're too dumb to know what a wonderful woman you are. That's why!"

I luxuriated in the soothing affection of his words. "Your Doris is a lucky woman."

He smiled, self-satisfied. "That she is. But I'll tell you one thing. She never met me at church. Never took me there either, except the day we got married."

"And I say that's your loss." I kept my voice light.

"My loss?" His voice was suddenly harsh. "Just tell me one thing, Kristie. What's God ever done for me? Huh? And what's he doing for your broken heart? Don't you hurt even though he's supposed to be loving you?"

I leaned forward and took his hand again. "God never promised to keep us from the problems and pains that everyone in the world has. All he promised to do was see us through the hurt, bear it with us, reassure us that we aren't alone. And that seems like a lot to me."

He sniffed. "You suffer from low expectations."

"Mr. Geohagan!"

"You'll never convince me that God cares. Never."

"Even though he gave his Son to die for you?"

"Rumor. Tradition. Lies."

I shook my head. "Truth."

He looked at me with pity. "I thought you were too intelligent to get taken in by some fool religion."

"Are you bored in here?" I asked.

"What?" He seemed thrown off balance by my change of topic.

"Bored, as in you don't have enough to do."

He frowned, unable to see where I was going. "Of course I'm bored."

"Then I've got a good project to fill some of your time. Read the Bible and check out God's claims and promises."

He looked less than excited with my idea. Boredom was obviously preferable. "I haven't got a Bible."

"Sure you do." I reached into his bedside table and pulled out a Gideon Bible. "I challenge you to read the Gospel of John. I'm going to get your papers for you. You read John for me."

He looked at me as though I suddenly tasted bad.

"It's better for you than your daily diet of soaps."

His lip curled in disgust. "No wonder that guy dumped you," he said. "You're too dictatorial."

I decided that maybe Doris wasn't so lucky after all.

SIXTEEN

There were pockets of time when I thought I'd die from the sharp pain that pierced my heart whenever I thought of Clarke. My breath would catch in my throat, and my eyes would fill.

Maybe I'm overreacting, I'd tell myself. Maybe I'm jumping to conclusions. Maybe there's nothing to be upset about. Maybe being kissed by a beautiful woman in the church parking lot doesn't mean a thing. After all, it could be a most trivial matter.

Then again, maybe it does mean something. Maybe it means a lot. Clarke isn't the type to go around kissing girls lightly. After all, he's a responsible Christian leader, a counselor and teacher. Maybe the problem's my conclusion jumping all right, but not in reference to him and her. In reference to him and me. I saw romance where there was none, affection where there was mere consideration. After all, when Nelson blasted him with that question, what could he say?

"May you be so lucky when you grow up."

All that statement proved was that Clarke was too polite to embarrass me in front of a repulsive child. If he really cared, he'd call or come see me.

He did neither.

I sighed. Now I knew what Todd was feeling. It served me right.

~ ~ ~ ~ ~

Surprisingly, the arrival of Isaiah at the farm was a great help to me. He turned out to be one of the most pleasant people I'd ever been around. He had an indefatigably positive outlook on life, and he shared his good spirits through an unending stream of practical jokes.

John had the dubious pleasure of having the salt shaker lid and all the salt fall into his morning oatmeal while Ruth giggled in delight at the cleverness of her betrothed.

Mary lifted the lid on one of her pots and found four severed chicken heads where there should have been gently stewing bodies.

I bit into an egg salad sandwich only to notice a strange taste. When I lifted the top slice of bread, I found one of Hawk's dog biscuits sogging amid the eggs. Everyone in the teachers' lunchroom thought the prank hilarious, but then they still had sandwiches to eat.

All this was within twenty-four hours of Isaiah's arrival.

Living with the gentle paranoia Ruth's intended induced might help keep thoughts of Clarke at bay, but I still thought it was a bit much when, the Monday evening before the wedding, I sat down at the kitchen table to talk to Mary and sat on Hawk's metal brush, bristles up, lying in wait for the unwary.

"Ruth thinks he's wonderful," said a sympathetic Mary, trying not to laugh as I rubbed my punctured anatomy. "They've driven me wild with worry on many occasions, but I'm hard pressed not to like him."

"Ruth should never be bored," I said, placing the offending brush in plain view lest someone else get similarly perforated.

Mary sat across from me. "Well, at least they're staying Plain. You probably don't understand how important that is to us, and I don't think I can begin to explain how thankful we are."

"I know how my parents would react if I turned my back on the Lord," I said, honored by Mary's openness.

She nodded. "Lately I've been so pleased to see Elam developing a real faith. I hope that in time Ruth and Isaiah will learn not just the Ordnung but the living faith beneath it."

I rested my elbows on the table after checking carefully for any other booby traps. "How do you define faith, Mary?"

She frowned in thought. "Well, there's Jesus, and there's the church. You believe in Jesus and keep the rules of the church, and you hope for the best. Of course it's very important to be separate from the world so you don't become worldly and proud."

"You believe not being worldly is important to salvation?"

"Oh, yes. Don't you? 'Be not conformed to this world.' You have to be obedient to the Ordnung to be redeemed."

"Then living your life properly is as important as believing in Jesus?"

"Living in harmony with the church is necessary," she said, not really answering my question.

"Which is why I can't become a Christian," said Jake as he rolled into the room. "As you both have undoubtedly noticed, the church and I aren't exactly in tune."

A spasm of deep pain shot across Mary's face.

Jake smiled amiably, either oblivious to his mother's distress or ignoring it. "Do we have any more root beer, Mom?"

"There's some in the refrigerator. Let me get it for you." She pushed herself up from the table and went to the refrigerator. She pulled out a bottle and brought it to him. Then, with tears in her eyes, she went upstairs.

I turned on Jake. "How long were you eavesdropping?" I asked sharply.

"Long enough. And don't scowl at me like that. I don't

make a habit of skulking around with my ear to the wall. I happened to be coming in and hesitated a minute to hear what you two had to say." He shrugged. "Discussions about religion interest me. I keep hoping that I'll learn something that allows a bit of leeway for a black sheep like me."

"Don't do that, Jake!"

He looked at me, startled. "Don't do what?"

"Hide behind the traditions of your family."

He watched me warily. "What do you mean?"

"You keep using your family's Amishness as an excuse for not becoming a Christian."

"What do you know about Amishness?" His voice was hard. "Do you think a couple of months on an Amish farm makes you an expert? You don't know anything about the pressure, the sermons, the rules."

"You're right; I don't. But you're missing my point. Being a Christian has nothing to do with traditions of any kind, no matter how much you love them or hate them. It has to do with a personal faith in Jesus as the Christ. Either you choose to believe in him or you don't."

"That's not what they say."

"See what I mean?"

"What?"

"You're hiding behind them."

"I am not," he defended himself angrily. "I'm just stating what they say."

"But the issue is what you say, Jake, not what they say. You can't spend your whole life saying it's everyone's fault but yours that you don't believe."

"Oh, no? Do you have any idea how tired I am of every-body telling me what I should believe? Like I'm not smart enough to reach any conclusions of my own! 'Jake, do this.'

'Jake, do that.' 'Jake, go to school.' 'Jake, believe in Jesus.' You'd think I lost my mind, not my legs! Even you get on me, and not just about religion!"

"Me?"

"You want me to meet this Rose person. I have enough trouble just getting through every day without meeting the person who saw me at my worst!"

I refused to sympathize. "See? You're doing it again. Everybody's picking on you, so it's their fault, not yours. It's even Rose's fault that you won't meet her because she happened to be indiscreet enough to be at the accident scene. I think you're hiding behind 'everybody' to avoid making any choice of your own."

"No wonder you and Jon Clarke make such a good couple," said Jake stiffly. "I'm surprised he's not here by your side to help you reel me into the kingdom."

The phone in his apartment rang, and we both looked in its direction, distracted. I pulled myself back to the subject at hand.

"That's unkind," I said, rising to cover the pain of his comment. "Clarke has nothing to do with this conversation. And another thing! You change subjects when you don't want to talk!"

"It sure beats leaving the room," he called after me as I ran upstairs. "Lecture, lecture, lecture, run. Shouldn't you be getting me on my knees? After you heal my legs, of course?"

What an awful person he can be, I thought as I threw myself across my bed. Nasty. Ugly. Why should I waste my time worrying about him when I could worry about me instead?

How proud Mom would have been of my mature, Christian attitude.

~ ~ ~ ~ ~

Tuesday was a bad day at school. I don't know whether the kids caught my distress and reacted to it or whether they would have been terrible even if I'd been singing "I'm a Happy, Happy Christian" all day.

A first-grader lost his lunch all over my desk, ruining my plan book and perfuming the room.

Two girls got in a hair-pulling, clothes-tearing fight over whose artwork was the best, and I got kicked and elbowed when I broke them up.

A troubled student took umbrage at an uncomplimentary comment from his neighbor about his unique, all-black painting, and I got there just in time to prevent his braining the other boy with a chair.

The mother of one of the girls in the fight came after school and harangued me for allowing her daughter to be attacked. I refrained, but barely, from giving her my opinion of the "darling girl."

When I finally arrived at Ripley's Storage Garage, I was in as snarly a state of mind as I'd ever been. It was already four forty-five and getting dark fast. Eastern Standard Time had returned over the weekend, and the earlier dusk was very evident between the rows of garages that made up the Ripley complex. As I drove through the gateway in the chain link fence, I was glad there were lights at regular intervals along the rows.

An older gentleman in the office gave me directions to Mr. Geohagan's unit, and I found it at the end of a long row of beige garages. I decided he had a thing for corner properties.

I parked my car in front of the unit, and in the illumination from a light on the wall three garages down I fitted the key into the lock and lifted the lightweight fiberglass door.

By feeling along the wall inside the door, I found a switch.

As light flooded the little room, a jumble of furniture, boxes, and miscellany sprang into view. I realized I was looking at the "sweeping up the heart," the ending of what had once been vibrant and alive and was now only a collection of dust-covered memories.

Lord, I don't know what you have in mind for me, but if it's possible, please don't let it be a hospital bed and a storage garage and nothing else.

Along the left wall was a small work area with a gray metal desk, a gooseneck lamp, a padded, ergonomically sound chair, two dinged-and-dreary gray file cabinets, and a very out-of-place navy leather easy chair.

The desk was awash with papers left by someone obviously planning to return soon. But he hadn't, and probably he never would.

Why did he work here in the discomfort of this garage instead of in his apartment? Certainly the apartment wasn't cheery, but it was better than this. And the leather chair—why keep it here instead of at home where he could lean back and read Max Brand?

I glanced over my shoulder at the gaping door as I began gathering up the papers. How dark it now looked out there. I felt uncomfortable, vulnerable. Maybe I should close the door. But then I'd have to open it again later, and my imagination would conjure all kinds of things just waiting for me.

"If I'm ever widowed," I once told my mother, "the first two things I'm going to buy are an electric garage door opener and an electric blanket."

Mom had only laughed. "Let's get you married before we worry about your being widowed."

But my comment was heartfelt, especially about the garage door opener. I hated going out at night when I had to lift our garage door on unseen darkness. Who knew what would be lurking there, just waiting for me. I hated just as much coming home, getting out to lift the door, pulling into the garage, and getting out again to lower the door. Talk about feeling defenseless. At the farm I parked out in the open, and it felt safer somehow.

I shivered now as I turned back to Mr. Geohagan's desk, and not from the cold. I stuffed all the papers into a large accordion folder that had obviously held them before. I was just reaching to open the left file drawer in the desk when the hair on the back of my neck began prickling. I made myself turn around.

In the doorway stood two men.

"What do you want?" I asked, my voice a mere whisper.

I looked from one to the other. They appeared ordinary. One had on a down vest and jeans and a Braves baseball cap—like millions of other men. The other had a neat haircut, and his rugby shirt could be seen beneath a fleecy anorak that looked straight out of L. L. Bean. Surely there was no reason to be afraid. They probably rented the garage next door.

But one wore a Braves cap. In Phillies territory.

"If you'll just get in your car and leave and make believe you've never been here today, we won't bother you at all," said the one in the anorak. "We have no quarrel with you."

"What?" It wasn't one of my better moments.

"Go. Get out. Leave. Now. And you won't get hurt."

"Just beat it out of here, lady." It was the man in the baseball cap.

He moved quickly toward me, and it was a flashback to the man—this very man?—rushing down the steps at me. I backed away instinctively, bumping into the low arm of the easy chair.

It caught me just behind the knees, and I fell backwards onto the soft cushions.

Before I could extricate myself, he was beside me, grabbing me, pushing me toward the door. I stared in fascination at his hand on my arm. It was covered with a lightweight plastic glove.

"Hi," said an unexpected voice.

We all spun toward the door.

The man from the office walked up to the garage and smiled brightly at me. "I just wanted to be certain you were all right back here before I went home for the day."

"She's fine," said the man in the anorak. "We got here just a few minutes ago to help her move some of these things."

"Funny," said the office man. "I didn't see you drive in."

"You were busy," said the man in the anorak reasonably. "We just drove on back. Don't worry about Kristie. We'll take care of her."

Somehow the words weren't comforting.

I smiled weakly at the office man, unable to open my mouth because of the paralyzing effect of the small, round object rammed into my back. The man in the Braves cap was actually holding a gun on me, and I'd heard a small click as he released its safety!

Suddenly hospital beds and storage garages and elderly ending of days looked very attractive.

The garage man waved cheerily and walked back into the night. As he disappeared from view, I felt I was losing my dearest friend.

"Good girl," said the man in the cap approvingly as he lowered the gun. He reached behind me and flicked off the light in the garage. The darkness wrapped around me, scaring me, making me jumpier than I already was.

"Too bright," he said. "Now get into your car and disappear. And don't bother to send the police or draw pictures for them or anything. We know exactly where to find you, all cozy at that crazy Amish place. And you'll regret it if we have to find you, believe me."

I believed him.

"Go!"

I started for the door, knowing that one or both of these men must be Mr. Stoltzfus's watchers. But why in the world would Cap and Anorak want to watch me?

But of course, it wasn't me. It was Mr. Geohagan's papers! I was important only because I led them to the papers. As were my room and my purse important as they might provide some clue—or key—to the same thing.

Mr. Geohagan worked here rather than in his apartment to protect a secret. I looked at the desk and the papers resting there. Why were they so valuable?

Anorak saw my look and gave a low, wicked chuckle. I had last heard that laugh on the other side of a closet door.

I looked away quickly so he wouldn't know I recognized him, or I might not drive away so easily. I concentrated on the man with the baseball cap as he bent to pick up some papers that had fallen on the floor. As he bent, the bill of his cap hit the edge of the desk, and the cap fell to the floor.

Another nonsurprise. Even though the light was faint, seeping into the garage from the lot lights, I easily recognized the man who had approached me in the woods Saturday. His cap, pulled down tight, had changed the lay of his ears to his head and covered his bald forehead. It had also made him look a little dim.

"Stupid," said Anorak. "Look at her face. She recognizes

you. I don't know whether it's from when she found you in the house or when you talked to her in the woods, but she can identify you."

Cap shrugged. "So what? She's not going to." He smiled at me, and all I could think of were beasts of prey, fangs dripping saliva in the moonlight.

"We can't let her go," said Anorak. "She'll draw your picture for the cops, maybe not this week or next, but eventually. And then she'll draw mine. She's like that, honest and all. They'll have you in no time. And then me."

They stared at me, obviously trying to decide what to do with me. I wanted to yell that I'd keep quiet forever if they'd just let me go. But I knew they were right. I would draw their pictures or identify them from those huge books of mug shots everyone always studied on cop shows. I was like that.

"They said no rough stuff," said the Braves man.

"So what?" said Anorak. "I'm in charge here, and I say we don't have a choice. We have to protect ourselves."

We were all quiet for a few minutes. I was too frightened to be thinking about much, but I knew they were considering ways to dispose of me.

"Gimme the gun," he said to Cap. His voice was so abrupt I jumped. He sneered at my fear as he held out his hand.

Cap hesitated.

"Give me the gun," Anorak repeated through clenched teeth.

I'd have given him my gun if I had one. In a nasty, evil way, there was something incredibly commanding about this man.

"But it's mine," Cap whined.

Anorak just stared, one eyebrow slightly raised above his glasses. If I could learn his trick, I could teach senior high, even junior high, any day.

Reluctantly Cap held out the gun.

Anorak took it casually and held it, safety still off, at his side. "Now back our car to the door so we can empty this stuff fast," he ordered. "We'll take care of her later."

As I stood with heart pounding and knees knocking, the Braves man, his cap back in position, turned their car around and opened the trunk. Casually he pulled out a tire iron, walked down three garages to the light, and broke the bulb.

"Better get the next one too," said Anorak.

In the disorienting darkness I heard another bulb shatter.

"No sense risking anyone seeing us now, is there? And don't you try going anywhere," he said, grabbing my arm. "The gun is still pointed at you."

The Braves guy lay the tire iron down, and in the faint illumination of the trunk light began emptying the desk and file cabinets. He lugged load after load as Anorak and I stood in the deep shadows and watched.

"Get every piece," Anorak ordered. "Every single scrap of paper."

"You could at least help," complained Cap.

"And leave her alone?"

"Then she can help."

Anorak shook his head, though I doubt Cap saw. "I like her where I know exactly what she's doing. Just cut your complaining and move it." He sighed as if he bore a great weight. "I can't wait to get away from you and your constant whining!"

"I am not whining!" shouted Cap. "I don't whine!" He spun and looked furiously at Anorak. As he did so, he lost his grip on the armload of papers he was carrying, and they showered to the ground. An errant breeze caught some of them, and they fanned out across the drive.

"Stupid!" yelled Anorak. He reached out to catch a few

sheets that fluttered in his direction.

As he reached, I pushed. I caught the man in the rump with my foot, and he toppled over on his face. His gun went flying, striking the ground and discharging.

Cap screamed, but I couldn't tell whether in pain or anger. I didn't wait to find out. I tore out the door and around the corner at the end of the line of garages into total blackness. I put my hands out in front of me and ran sightlessly. Any risk was better than standing around docilely, waiting to get shot. My back itched as I kept expecting the smash of a bullet between my shoulders.

I flew around the second corner and felt true terror as I ran headlong into the grip of a third man.

SEVENTEEN

My heart stopped as a hand clapped firmly over my mouth.

"Don't make a sound," a voice whispered in my ear.

I couldn't have spoken if my life depended on it.

"Run!" the familiar voice whispered.

Like I needed to be told.

I fled willingly behind the sprinting figure. We rounded one corner, then another, zigzagging through the rows of garages.

Now that I was back in the main part of the complex, the little lights on the garages showed us the way. Of course, they would also show the bad guys the way.

Shouts and shots followed us as Anorak and Cap gave chase, but we always managed to be at least a corner ahead. Even so, my back twitched and I imagined the staggering impact of a bullet tearing through muscle and bone, piercing the heart, *my* heart.

Look, Ma, I'm shot.

We stopped to catch our breath in the shadows of a rented moving van parked before a storage unit. The man turned and held out his arms, and I saw that it was Clarke. I buried my face in his chest and clung weakly. My legs were like spaghetti, and my heart hammered in my ears. I'd never been so terrified and so happy in my life.

"What are you doing here?" I panted. Not that I really cared how or why he had come. I was just glad he was here!

"Are you all right?" he said into my hair. His arms were a

steel vise clamping us together. All the worries and conjectures of the last two days fell away.

A shout from Anorak sounded just around the corner, and Clarke and I broke apart. I made a strange little hiccupy noise as I swallowed a scream.

He grabbed my hand, and we dived to the ground together, rolling under the moving van. We lay huddled in the middle, arms wrapped around each other. Under any other circumstances, it would have been my current version of heaven to be so entwined, but all I could think was, *Lord, don't let any feet be hanging out, okay?*

"You check down this aisle," yelled Anorak to Cap. He was mere yards away. "I'll go to the gate to make sure she doesn't get out there. We can't let her escape!"

Footsteps thundered toward us and came to a stop beside the truck. I stared at a pair of black-and-white sneakers just inches from my face, as mesmerized by them as a cobra is by the charmer's music. The heels were toward me, and I could see that he had run the left one down pretty badly. Bad hip? Who cared?

I was afraid to breathe, though Cap was puffing so hard he probably wouldn't have heard me if I had a sneezing fit.

The sneakers turned to face the truck. The toes were scuffed, and one lace was undone. Maybe he'd trip the next time he ran. Of course that might mean that we were also running, having been discovered down here.

Nah. We were safe in our clever hideaway, especially from a great genius like him.

"Okay," yelled Cap. "Come out of there!"

I flinched as if he'd hit me, and I felt Clarke go rigid beside me. How had he known? A reasoned guess? Maybe I'd underestimated him. Or maybe it was just luck? Or was something hanging out after all? A foot? A jacket?

Oh, Lord, please, no!

The black-and-white sneakers walked right up to my nose, and I squeezed my eyes shut on the if-I-can't-see-him-he-can't-see-me premise.

"Out!" Cap ordered. And he yanked the door of the truck cab open.

Clarke and I sagged with relief.

Thank you, Lord!

Cap swore as he slammed the door shut and swung his tire iron into the side of the truck just inches from my head, not once but twice. The clanging of metal on metal at close quarters reverberated inside my head.

I thought of the poor people who had rented the truck. They would have a hard time explaining those dents to the rental company.

"Honest! We didn't do it. When we came back in the morning, they were just there."

"Sure, mister. That's what they all say. It's a real shame you didn't take the insurance we offered you."

Cap stood beside the moving van a minute, listening. We held our breath and prayed. Then he turned away and rounded a corner.

Relief made my ears buzz. In the warm flush of temporary safety I thought I would be happy just lying here all night beside Clarke. Surely the men would decide to go with the revealing light of morning, and everything would return to normal, whatever that was.

Clarke tightened his arm around me and pulled me close.

"We're going up," he whispered in my ear. "It's too dangerous here!"

Up? Up? How could we go up?

He rolled out from under the truck, and I followed. He climbed onto the vehicle's hood, reached down, and pulled me up after him.

I cringed at the pop and crack of the metal underfoot. Surely Cap would hear, would come flying around the corner and catch us midclimb. The thought of his tire iron across my shins made me twitch uncontrollably.

"Hurry!" I whispered, as if Clarke needed my encouragement.

He clambered up the windshield to the roof of the cab, then onto the roof of the truck body, and I climbed right after him. In a quick surge of movement he was on the garage roof. He turned to give me a hand, but I was already crouched on the roof beside him.

Suddenly Anorak raced down the passage below us, and we fell flat. A small cloud of dust rose about us as years of accumulated roof dirt was disturbed. I fought the urge to sneeze by rubbing my nose like mad.

"Did you hear that?" Anorak hissed.

Cap limped behind him, winded and unhappy. "What?" he gasped. "I didn't hear nothing."

Anorak snorted. "Of course you didn't. How could you? You're panting too hard to hear anything. Aaugh! I can't stand it! Why do they keep making me work with you? You drive me crazy!"

"Don't do that, Marty," Cap snarled. "Don't push me."

"Put that tire iron down, you idiot." Marty's voice dripped with condescension. "I don't got time for your macho nonsense. We got to find that girl. Besides—" there was a lengthy pause, and I could just picture them, each trying to stare the other down—"don't forget that I've got the gun."

There was a moment of tense silence, and then Cap must

have blinked, I heard Marty snort derisively.

"You go that way," he said. "I'll meet you at the entrance."

Clarke and I stayed still until both men were some distance away. Then, bending low, we moved cautiously along the flat, shadowy roof away from our erstwhile ladder. At the far end of the building, we lay huddled in a darkness deepened by the entrance lights below. I listened in heart-stopping tension as Marty and Cap ran up and down the rows below us.

Dear Lord, don't let them think to look up! They're not in the mood to be kind.

When they stopped immediately beneath us, I squeezed my eyes shut and ducked my head. Clarke's arm tightened around me. Once again we were afraid to breathe.

"Maybe she got out after all," said Cap. He was gasping, speaking only two or three words at a time, sounding as bad as Mr. Geohagan. The man needed an exercise program desperately.

"She didn't get out." Fury filled Marty's voice. "I would have seen her. And she didn't scale the fence, not with that barbed wire around the top of it. No, she's here somewhere, and we'd better find her. There are a couple of stored RVs in the back. Look in them."

"I already did. She's not there."

"Well, look under them."

And they were off.

I leaned close to Clarke's ear. What a nice ear. And he smelled good too. "You sure called that one right," I whispered. "If we'd stayed under that truck, they'd have gotten us in time."

I felt him smile. "I've got to tell you," he whispered in my ear, "when I heard those lights break and then that shot, my heart stopped." His voice shook at the memory. "Try not to do that to me again, okay?"

When he kissed me, I melted against him. Most appropriately, bells and whistles sounded, accompanying the fireworks exploding in my head.

No, not bells and whistles. More like sirens. I pulled back. "What's that?"

"The cops," he said.

"Where'd they come from?"

"We called them."

"We did?"

"Not you-and-me we. Mary Ann-and-me we. And the attendant." He leaned over to kiss me again.

I put a hand to his chest. "Mary Ann? Who's Mary Ann?" I just bet she was blonde and cute and had an umbrella.

Below there was shouting, running, cursing, and searchlights were blazing. A shot, then two, tore the night.

Cap yelled, "Don't shoot! Don't shoot! I didn't do nothin'!"

"Shut up," Marty bellowed at him. "We'll be out by morning! They got nothing on us!"

The confusion below was nothing compared to the confusion I felt. My knight had come to my rescue, but he had brought along Mary Ann?

That wasn't in the script.

I started to get up. No more coziness on the roof for me.

"Get down here!" Clarke grabbed me none too gently and pulled me back.

I lost my balance and fell on him. Accidentally my elbow caught him in the gut. I tried to feel bad as he wheezed, "Dangerous. Bullets."

I rested my head on his chest and listened to his two-timing heartbeat. "How did you know to come here?" I asked in what I hoped was a cool, detached manner.

"I went to the Zooks'," he said, "and Mary told us you

might be here. We arrived just as the attendant was leaving. He told us you and your two friends were in the garage at the end of the third line. You've had too many strange things happening to you recently. As soon as he mentioned friends, I got worried. I asked if one of them was wearing a baseball cap, and the attendant said, 'Yeah, a Braves cap.' And then the lights were broken. I told Mary Ann and the attendant to call the cops, and I took off to see if you were all right. When the shot was fired, I almost died."

"I was doing okay," I said with a distinct lack of appreciation for his emotional turmoil and gracious rescue effort.

"That you were," he agreed magnanimously, kissing me on the top of my head.

Suddenly we noticed that it was quiet below.

A woman's voice rang out. "Clarke! Jon Clarke! Where are you?"

"Mary Ann," he told me needlessly.

"Oh, great, I'm so glad."

He didn't even hear my sarcasm.

We got to our feet and leaned over the roof. We watched as people in blue scurried up and down the rows, looking strangely out of perspective. Red and blue lights flashed, and a pair of men in handcuffs were put in a panda car. The attendant and a blonde stood off to the side looking worried. The woman was wringing her lovely hands while the attendant patted her on the back to comfort her.

"Up here!" yelled Clarke. "Up here!"

I was vaguely aware of a ladder being placed against the building, vaguely aware of climbing down it. All I could see was the little curly-haired blonde, whose face lit up when she saw Clarke in one piece. She pointed and jumped up and down and clapped her hands, and I hated myself for my jealousy.

210

"I was so worried about you!" she shouted as she rushed forward. She threw her arms around Clarke as soon as his feet hit the ground, kissing him with obvious affection, looking far more lovely than worried.

I didn't even want to think about what I looked like, rolling around on the ground under trucks, lying on dirty roofs. Some comparisons are too painful.

"Mary Ann, I want you to meet Kristie." Clarke smiled from one of us to the other.

Mary Ann smiled charmingly at me.

I tried to smile back. I wondered if I looked as pickled as I felt.

"I'm so glad to meet you!" she gushed. "Clarke told—"

"Excuse me, Miss Matthews, but we need to speak with you a few minutes." It was one of the policemen. He took me by the arm and led me gently but firmly to his car. I looked back over my shoulder at Clarke and shrugged. I hoped I looked properly disappointed, like what-can-you-do? In reality I felt so relieved to be out of a situation I wasn't certain I could handle that I wanted to hug the cop.

"Just sit right down and tell me what happened here tonight," he said briskly. Brisk was good. I could deal with brisk. It was kindness and sympathy I didn't think I could handle.

Another officer began talking to Clarke and Mary Ann and the attendant. As if in a daze, I heard Mary Ann say, "But if we don't leave now, Clarke, we'll miss our plane." She turned to the officer they had been talking to. "I haven't been home in over a year, and our plane leaves in an hour and a half."

"Kristie," Clarke called as Mary Ann pulled on his arm.

I smiled sweetly at him and turned my back, giving my full attention to my interview. It was preferable to murdering him and/or Mary Ann in full view of the authorities.

EIGHTEEN

I drove to Holiday House on my way home from school the next day, Wednesday. I walked up the front walk past the great copper beech with its masses of golden leaves gracefully bending to touch the ground. Clusters of lavender, crimson, and gold chrysanthemums brightened the front porch and sat in brass pots in the lobby. Heavy brass chandeliers hung from the ceiling, casting a warm glow over the green-and-wine upholstered furniture and oriental rugs.

Holiday House was a beautiful facility. When the time came for me to go to a care facility, I sure wouldn't mind coming here. If I could ever afford it. I couldn't even begin to imagine how expensive it was, especially for someone with a private room like Mr. Geohagan's.

I found him sitting in bed surrounded by reams of paper.

"Kristie!" he said when he saw me. "Are you really all right? They didn't hurt you, did they? And the police treated you with respect? The press didn't bother you?"

I shook my head. "I'm fine," I assured him. Not happy. Not excited about life. Not ever planning to laugh again. But also not physically harmed. Fine.

"The police told me what happened when they brought me my material this morning." He laid a protective hand on the stack of innocent-looking papers resting on his stomach.

I stared somewhat resentfully at the papers. What was in them that made those unknown men take such extreme action? And what could possibly be worth putting me in such jeopardy—not just last night but several times?

Mr. Geohagan saw me staring at them and misunderstood. "These aren't the originals," he said. "They're copies. The police need the originals for evidence against those guys. They said you made a great ruckus until they made copies for me and promised to deliver them." He grinned at me. "I'm proud of you. I just wish I'd seen you in action."

It was a good thing he hadn't seen me last night. I had behaved quite badly. I'd been upset about Clarke—massive understatement—and I focused all that distress on the poor policemen who had to deal with me. I think I even cried a bit over how important it was to get those papers to the poor dying man to whom they belonged.

"He was counting on me," I had said with exaggerated histrionics. "Please don't let it look like I've disappointed him. He has no one else in the whole world!"

In retrospect it was enough to make me gag.

Mr. Geohagan took my hand in his thin, dry one. He patted me gently. "I spent the last couple of days worrying about you," he said. "First there was that louse, What's-his-name, and then those terrible men last night!"

My eyes filled with tears, and I was touched by his palpable concern, a balm on my raw spirit.

"I'll be fine," I said. I tried to smile reassuringly, but I gave up the effort. "Eventually anyway. I'm sad right now, but I'm strong, you know. I certainly don't plan to do anything like Cathleen, either on purpose or accidentally. I plan to depend on God to help me get through it all."

Some of Mr. Geohagan's solicitude faded.

"Don't go clouding up at the mere mention of God," I said. "You look like a thundercloud trying to find the energy to crack the skies open."

"That bad?"

I nodded. "Worse."

We sat in companionable silence for a few minutes.

Finally I said, "Well, I got your papers for you. Did you read the Gospel of John for me?"

"Believe it or not, I did. It was kind of interesting."

I think I hid my surprise. "How was it interesting?"

He cleared his throat self-consciously. "I wasn't aware that Jesus was so outspoken about himself: 'I'm the Bread of Life. I'm the Lamb of God. I'm the only Way to God.' I thought men had made all those things up because they wanted them to be true. Of course, maybe they still did. After all, Jesus didn't write the Gospel. John could say anything he wanted."

I nodded. "Sure, John or others could have made those things up, but would they then die for things they knew were lies?"

"Maybe the disciples and all didn't lie. Maybe they told the truth as they knew it. Maybe Jesus lied," Mr. Geohagan said. "Maybe he's no more God than the nut on the corner."

I nodded again. "Could be. But would people die for someone who was a liar or a nut? Or live for one either?"

"People are notoriously gullible. There's always a group following some demented guru somewhere."

"True, but those cults always die out, sometimes by their own hands. We're talking about millions of people over a period of two thousand years when we talk about all those who have followed Jesus."

He looked at me. "You obviously think he was telling the truth."

I nodded. "I do."

He pulled a piece of paper off one of the piles on his bed and turned his attention ostentatiously to it. "I'm not so sure myself. Maybe I'm just not as trusting as you." He grabbed a second sheet of paper. "I need to think about it more."

I recognized the finality in his tone. There would be no more talk about God or Jesus today. That was all right. I would allow him to set the pace. It wasn't my job to change his heart, just to help him consider.

I reached in my new handbag for a paperback and settled to read as though I still had the ability to concentrate. Hah! All I saw when I looked at the page was a beautiful blonde with her arms wrapped around Clarke's neck.

Oh, Lord, how did this happen? How did I get so emotionally involved?

I turned a page so Mr. Geohagan would think I really was reading.

How did I misunderstand Clarke so? Am I really that stupid? And how will I live without him? More to the point, at least at this moment, how will I ever get out of here without dissolving into tears and upsetting Mr. Geohagan?

There was a knock on the door, and a young man with the strangest shape I'd ever seen entered. His legs seemed to begin under his armpits, and he looked like he had no chest. I studied him, wondering where he kept his heart and lungs and other thoracic items.

He nodded politely at me but turned his attention to Mr. Geohagan. "I think you wanted to see me?"

"Ah. Yes, yes, yes. Come in. Come in."

His enthusiasm made me study the unusual man even more.

Looking hopeful, the strangely shaped man oozed to the side of the bed without seeming to move, an impressive accomplishment considering that he was all legs.

"Kristie, I don't mean to be impolite, but I must talk to this young man for a while." Mr. Geohagan smiled apologetically.

"I understand." I got quickly to my feet and waved a friendly farewell. "I'll see you later."

I left Holiday House and drove home, back into all the chaos and excitement of the Zook wedding. I sighed as I climbed out of my car.

What ironic timing, Lord. My world is falling apart while Ruth is building hers. I'm glad for her, Lord. I really am. I want her and Isaiah to be as happy as any couple ever was. But does everything have to be so awful for me?

I went upstairs and lay on my crimson-and-blue quilt, where I stared miserably at the ceiling. When a stray tear began rolling across my cheek into my hair, I turned on my side and let it be absorbed by the quilt. I shivered, then twisted and turned a bit until the quilt was covering me. Then I curled on my side again, trying to get warm.

I shall stay here forever, Lord, curled in this tight little ball of pain. You don't mind, do you?

Even if the Lord didn't mind, which I suspected he did, I knew that eventually Mr. Edgars, my principal, would. He had this thing about his teachers coming to work. I sighed deeply, a melancholy and self-pitying habit I'd always detested.

I'll break it, Mom. I promise. Someday. When I'm happy again. If I ever am. Just don't wave that finger in my face. This isn't buck-up-my-girl time.

I sighed again. Between thoughts of Mom and Mr. Edgars, my wallowing had lost its flavor. I might as well get up and go eat dinner—if I could swallow. I pulled myself upright and went downstairs to see who was here now.

Relatives I had never seen before had been visiting all week, helping with preparations and offering good wishes, and the festive air had intensified as the wedding day grew closer. A new Amish family was about to be established, and the whole community recognized the importance of this fact.

With tomorrow the big day, the shed bulged with food, provision had been made to stable all the horses expected, and the big downstairs room had been emptied of all its everyday furniture.

"How long will this wedding last?" I asked Jake. "The actual ceremony, I mean."

He sat in the doorway to his apartment, and I sat on the bottom step leading to my rooms. We were a little pocket of calm in the whirlwind that had been sweeping the house since daybreak.

The men were killing and cleaning chickens, ducks, and turkeys. The women were baking pies, making dressing to stuff the fowl, and peeling enough potatoes to feed my entire school. The men also emptied the garbage and built temporary tables for the wedding feast. These tables now lined the entire downstairs room. The house was redolent with the scent of onions, celery, and spices.

"The service will take three to four hours," Jake said stiffly. He was still slightly angry with me over my accusation the other night that he hid behind others. Or maybe it was from the suggestion that he meet Rose. I didn't have the energy to figure it out right now. Maybe later.

"Four hours?" I stared at him with no enthusiasm. "I'm used to sitting still for thirty-five or forty minutes for a sermon at most. Four hours is a bit long, isn't it?"

Jake nodded. "And wait until Old Amos gives his sermon." He shook his head. "He says the same thing every time. The same thing. Not that you'll understand." He looked at me. "It'll all be in High German."

Four hours of High German. Maybe I should just go to

school after all and show up in time for the feast.

Ruth gave a sudden peal of laughter at something Isaiah said, and as I watched them, I knew I wouldn't miss this wedding for anything. Not only was I curious, but I liked Ruth and her practical joker very much.

"What will this Old Amos say that I won't understand?" I asked Jake.

"He always talks about Noah. He used to do Sarah and Abraham until finally someone told him that he always said the same thing. So he switched, and now he always says the same thing about Noah."

"What does he say?"

"He talks about how corrupt Noah's world was and how Noah and his family followed God and how God kept them safe through the flood. So everyone should be certain they have a family that follows God, and he'll keep them safe through the floods of life."

I nodded. "That doesn't sound too bad."

Jake shrugged, forgetting to be angry. "It takes him at least a half hour to say it."

I laughed. "How about your father? Does he speak?"

"Always. But he tries to tailor his comments to the couple marrying, and he works hard to be short and to the point."

"That's not surprising," I said as Jake's phone sounded in the distance. "Your father's a very fine man."

Jake stiffened suddenly, looked at me as if he'd never seen me, and wheeled into his rooms without a word. He shut his door firmly behind him.

I sat, confused, thinking back over what I'd just said. How could I have upset him by saying his father was a nice man?

I went upstairs feeling as dynamic as melted ice cream.

~~~~~

I didn't feel much better the next morning as I dressed for the wedding, but the excitement was catching as soon as I came downstairs. Ruth and Isaiah and their two attending couples had already left for the Stoltzfus farm where the ceremony was to take place, but the Zook farm was bustling with last-minute activity. I was surprised to learn that John and Mary probably wouldn't go to the wedding. They would be too busy with the duties of preparation and hosting.

It seemed very sad to me that John wouldn't get to preach at his own daughter's wedding. My mother would die before she missed my wedding—if and when I ever had one. And Dad had big plans to give his baby away, even though he always teased about holding the ladder so my groom and I could elope.

"Won't Ruth and Isaiah feel bad if your parents aren't there?" I asked Jake as he drove me to the Stoltzfus farm. He made no reference to his abrupt leaving last night, but his stiffness had returned.

He shook his head. "Parents often don't go to the wedding. They're just too busy with last-minute preparations for the feasting. Everybody understands."

I shrugged mentally as I took a seat on the back bench in the women's section and watched the festival of Amish life swirl around me. Several of the women whom I'd met previously nodded shyly to me and smiled. I was relieved to see I wasn't the only English guest, but we were definitely a minority. I saw Andy and Zeke slip into seats beside Jake. It was warming to see the brothers shake hands with obvious affection. The rest of the English family including daughters-in-law and grandchildren sat near me in the back. Though they were relatives, this was a community day, and none of us were part of the community.

Ruth and Isaiah sat on the front row with their attending couples. One by one the district ministers rose and gave their sermons on the responsibilities and privileges of marriage. Just as Jake had warned, Old Amos rambled on and on. By contrast, the others spoke briefly and forcefully. I had no idea what any of them said, but everyone listened carefully and nodded their heads.

I thought of the last wedding I had attended, that of my college roommate. There had been flowers and music, and Mandie had worn yards of lace. The groomsmen wore morning coats, and the bridesmaids, including me, were resplendent in a gorgeous shade of teal and carried nosegays with trailing ivy. We purposely and boldly called attention to ourselves, dressing extravagantly for the special occasion.

By contrast, Ruth and Isaiah were dressed much as they were any other day except that everything they wore was new. Ruth had told me that she would take the fresh white kapp and apron she was wearing and pack them away, not wearing them again until her burial, but Isaiah's shirt and pants and hat would join his wardrobe as Sunday clothes.

My back hurt, and my seat was asleep before the service was half over, but I tried not to squirm, especially since the children around me were sitting so quietly. One mother near me touched her fidgeting three-year-old, and he immediately stilled. A small piece of whoopie pie was his reward.

Suddenly all I wanted in this world was a whoopie pie.

When the service finally ended, everyone headed for the Zook farm. Jake and I arrived first, and he pulled as far out of the way as he could. The rest of the family parked off the farm and walked over.

Soon buggy after buggy turned into the drive. The horses were quickly released from the shafts and led to the makeshift barn where they were tethered, fed, and watered. The buggies filled the drive, a sea of gray enclosures and black wheels.

The men gathered in groups to talk and tell stories, their black felt hats firmly in place. The teenagers eyed each other in the manner of teens of any culture, and the little children played tag, working off some of their contained energy. The women, chattering and laughing, gravitated to the kitchen and the final preparations for serving the food.

As I watched the press of people, I felt very much apart. I wanted only to be alone. I needed to be alone. All the camaraderie and love was more than I could deal with at the moment.

I slipped upstairs and traded my heels for a pair of flats. I hoped Ruth didn't see me leave, but I doubted it would register if she did. The scores of people milling around gossiping, telling stories, and eating made it impossible to know who was doing what or going where.

I walked slowly down the road to Aunt Betty Lou and Uncle Bud's where I'd parked my car. It was a crisp November day, sunny and bright. The branches were largely bare, the flowers dead, shriveled by the sharp snap of frost last week. It was the beginning of the stark season.

I got in my car and drove aimlessly for a while, then found myself at Holiday House.

Well, why not? I parked and went up to Mr. Geohagan's room.

When I walked in, he was busy talking to the guy with no chest, the one who had visited him yesterday. They were examining some of the papers Mr. Geohagan had spread all over the bed.

They stopped talking as soon as I walked into the room, looking at me as if I'd caught them at something illegal. Mr.

Geohagan frowned, and the strange man stared as though he couldn't believe I had been so tactless as to come in. I felt thirteen years old, the awkward, inept intruder who wanted to be part of the gang but who would never be accepted.

I blinked in surprise. What was happening here? The strange man was the one who didn't belong, not me. I'd risked my life for this old man. I was his true and loyal friend. Wasn't I?

Mr. Geohagan waved his hand dismissively at me. "Another time, Kristie," he said abruptly.

"Sure," I said and left.

I told myself all the way down the hall that the tears stinging my eyes were foolish, that Mr. Geohagan hadn't meant to hurt my feelings, that I was just supersensitive right now. And while I knew I was right, I still had to blink like crazy to keep the tears from spilling over and streaming down my cheeks.

If I didn't count stray tears, which I didn't, I hadn't cried about Clarke yet. I knew that when I did, it wouldn't be a pretty sight. When I cry, my skin gets blotchy and my nose turns red. My face scrunches up in a pathetic mask. If and when I cried, I'd better be alone.

In the lobby I picked up the last copy of the day's *Intelligencer*. I looked at the front page as much to protect my wobbling self-control as to see what was going on in the world.

A supremely confident Adam Hurlbert, the perfect candidate, smiled at me from under an astonishing headline: ACCUSATIONS HURLED AT HURLBERT: WOULD-BE SENATOR CITED FOR TAX EVASION.

NINETEEN

I read the article in disbelief.

Adam Hurlbert, Pennsylvania's front-runner for the United States Senate, has been accused of tax evasion.

The Intelligencer has turned over to police evidence uncovered by this reporter that documents these charges.

Included in the evidence is a record of Hurlbert's personal expenses for the years 1980–1996. The record clearly shows Hurlbert spending money far in excess of his declared income for these same years. Receipts for many extravagant purchases—"the tip of the iceberg," says an unidentified source—are included as proof of the charges.

Also included in the evidence turned over to the police is a detailed financial statement purporting to show that when Hurlbert Construction contracted or subcontracted with firms, Adam Hurlbert inevitably made large personal investments in the stock market or large deposits in banks outside the country. The timing of these financial transactions is, at best, suspect.

Authorities will investigate the possibility of kickbacks.

Hurlbert's local campaign headquarters refuses to comment on the story, saying only that the candidate and his wife, Irene, are in western Pennsylvania soliciting last-minute support for Tuesday's election.

I looked up in shock. "He's a crook. I can't believe it. Adam Hurlbert's an out-and-out crook!"

I must have spoken aloud because a man walking by said, "Can you believe it? And I was going to vote for the guy!"

"Me, too." I held out the paper. "Do you think it's all true?"

"Do you think they'd print it if it weren't? The evidence must be pretty solid, or they'd never risk the legal consequences."

The man shuffled off to his unknown business, and I walked slowly to my car.

Poor Irene! What must it be like to wake up one morning and find you're married to a criminal!

I cocked an eyebrow. If she didn't already know.

I actually felt sorry for Nelson, the poor little twit, and I was glad when he didn't come to school the next day. It was going to be bad enough for him without having the kids rag on him about his stepfather. How the mighty are fallen.

The accusations were the talk of the teachers' room, and everyone was as anxious as I for the next installment of the story. To this point, TV and radio reports merely repeated the *Intell*'s claims, though not for long, I was sure. It was only a matter of time before the *Intell*'s evidence was available to all.

The Intelligencer and its next scoop hit the streets about the time I began my afternoon classes, so I didn't see it until after school. What I found took my breath away.

HURLBERT CAUSES GIRL'S DEATH: CANDIDATE DESERTED YOUNG LOVER FOR IRENE. Staring out at me was a picture of Adam Hurlbert and a lovely young woman identified as Cathleen Geohagan.

I stared at the photo. No wonder her father had said I didn't look like her. She was gorgeous.

The Intelligencer has learned that Pennsylvania's home-and-family candidate for the United Stated Senate, Adam Hurlbert, 52, was involved in a love affair last year with Cathleen Geohagan, 21. When he left her without warning for Irene Parsons Carmody, the widowed daughter of Pennsylvania governor Benjamin Parsons, Geohagan collapsed. A short time later she took her life by mixing alcohol and prescription drugs.

Not only did Hurlbert's attachment to Irene Carmody lead to the death of Cathleen Geohagan, but the shock of Geohagan's tragic death caused her mother, Doris Geohagan, 62, to suffer a massive stroke. Mrs. Geohagan lives today comatose in a nursing home with no hope for recovery.

The girl's bereaved father, Everett Geohagan, 65, now childless and a virtual widower, shared with this reporter from his nursing-home bed his great and continuing sorrow that a man capable of such cruel and immoral behavior seeks to be elected to one of the highest offices in our land. "Dare we trust a man who behaved as Adam Hurlbert did?" Everett Geohagan asks. "His opportunistic transfer of affections killed my daughter."

Another article on the front page, a follow-up to the previous day's tax-evasion story, was an account of Hurlbert's arrest. He had surrendered to authorities at his home upon his return from Pittsburgh the previous evening. Accompanying the story were pictures of the police at the door of the Hurlbert home and of Hurlbert in the backseat of a police car, drawn and defeated. There was even a picture of Irene looking brave and loyal, with poor, bewildered Nelson by her side.

"The party is in disarray," said the article. I laughed. I bet it was.

When I finished reading, I crumbled the *Intell* and stared ahead blankly.

So Mr. Geohagan—for he had to be the source of all this information—had gotten his revenge for the wrongs he felt Hurlbert had done him and his family.

But at what a price!

He had smeared his daughter's reputation.

He had paraded his ill and defenseless wife.

He had endangered my life—not once but repeatedly—a fact he conveniently neglected to tell anyone.

Everything he'd done since I met him was meant first to protect, then retrieve those precious papers so he could give them to—I searched the paper for the byline on the articles—Barnum Hadley. The man with no chest.

The attempted and actual purse snatchings, the watchers at the farm, the man on the stairs, the man in the woods, the night in the closet, the flight for my life at the storage garage—all were because of Mr. Geohagan.

I opened the paper again and studied the picture of Irene. Standing next to her was a tall, anorexic man identified as William Bozner, Adam Hurlbert's campaign manager. He was the man with Adam the night of the rally and robbery at Park City. He was also, I realized now, the man I had seen visiting Mr. Geohagan, the man to whom Mr. Geohagan had pledged his trust.

"You can trust me, Bill," Mr. Geohagan had said.

Hah!

Somewhere along the line the Hurlbert forces had found cause to distrust Mr. Geohagan. Why? What had happened? I had no idea, but with that distrust came fear. Did this old man have proof of Adam's financial shenanigans? Would he do anything with it? If so, what?

First they searched his apartment, as I knew only too well, but all they found was me. Their concern intensified, as did their need for information. Since Mr. Geohagan was confined because of illness, they began following the one with ready access to him, the one who ran his errands, mailed his letters, and sat with him by the hour. Me.

And did Mr. Geohagan warn me? No. He knowingly allowed me to remain in danger.

The hurt and disappointment I felt were so overwhelming I wanted to bawl. I had poured hours of care and prayer into this man, and all I got was a knockout punch in my emotional nose.

And I'd felt so guilty when I let the presence of the key slip to Jake and Clarke! How he must have laughed!

Lord, how could he do this to me? It's not fair!

I wadded the paper into a ball and tossed it at the wastebasket. It bounced off the edge and fell to the floor. I felt like kicking it, stomping it, attacking the messenger for the message.

"Child, how could he do this to me?"

The thought moved across my consciousness as lightly as the breath of God, and it stopped me cold in my poor-me tracks. I wasn't the only one hurt by Mr. Geohagan's great need for vengeance. I was just the one who suffered from self-pity.

I sighed deeply, walked sadly to my car, the last one remaining in the school lot, and drove slowly to Holiday House.

One hard question kept racing through my mind. As I pondered it, I drove automatically. I think I stopped at the proper stop signs and red lights. I think I obeyed the speed limit. I think I stayed in my lane and ran over no errant pedestrians.

The question: Was I sorry I had given so much time and care to Mr. Geohagan?

Mom would have been proud of me because I wasn't thinking poor-me anymore. Rather, I was considering my motives. What had compelled me to return again and again to visit him? Why was I willing to mail his letters and run his errands, to hold his hand and talk about my private life, to encourage him and let him encourage me?

The answer was very important because it would show me a lot about myself. Did I do these things out of pity or sympathy for a lonely old man? Did I do them to show everybody what a nice person I was? Did I do them so people would *tell* me what a nice person I was? Did I do them because he needed somebody, and I was willing to be that somebody? Did I do it because I wanted to model God's love to him?

All of the above, I had to admit. A mixture of motives at best. The trouble was, now I knew that the object of my sympathy and concern wasn't worth it. I knew that being nice, at least in this case, was just a synonym for being dumb, for being taken advantage of, for being manipulated and being too naive to realize it.

But he did need you, that soft voice whispered into my anger and bitterness. *He does need you. You did the right thing. Being taken advantage of is not the worst thing in the world.*

Hah! I yelled as I shut my ears to the breath of God and elbowed my way self-righteously through the TV crews and newsprint reporters clogging the front lawn of Holiday House. Hah!

And just how long would it be before these people wrote about Kristie Matthews, the dumb and gullible enabler that Mr. Geohagan deployed to accomplish his plans, even from his hospital bed? I could hardly wait for the embarrassment and invasion of privacy.

Only by waving down a passing nurse who had seen me several times before was I able to talk my way past the police guard at the front door.

"You need a list of regular visitors," I said tartly, just before I let the door slip shut in the officer's face. "Some of us are important around here."

He pushed the door open and called politely after me as I stalked down the hall, "A list is being drawn up now, miss." He smiled sweetly as he withdrew his head.

I ground my teeth. I hated being one-upped.

I burst into Mr. Geohagan's room full of rationalized and justified feelings of betrayal. Did I have a speech planned for him! It'd burn his ears, flay his skin, pull out his emotional fingernails.

I stopped short at the sight of the wizened old man lying in the bed, eyes closed, oxygen cannula at his nose. Somehow, in the time since I'd realized what he'd done, in my mind he'd grown two heads and begun to breathe fire. He was an unrepentant Darth Vader, the evil Ming the Merciless.

But he wasn't a monster. He was a sick old man who looked worse than ever. And he needed me more than ever whether he realized it or not.

Oh, God, help me! Help me see him as you do.

He must have sensed my presence, for he opened his eyes, saw me, and smiled.

"I was afraid you'd never come back," he whispered.

"I came to yell at you," I said as I walked to the bed. "I don't think I've ever been so upset."

"Not even over What's-his-name?"

"Different ball game. Today you hurt more than he does,

and that's no small accomplishment."

"I had to tell, you know," he said earnestly. "It wouldn't be fair to people to let them elect Adam. You understand that, don't you?"

I shook my head. "No, I don't. And please, Mr. Geohagan. Don't condescend to me by making false claims of altruism. If you were really concerned about justice and fairness for the people and all those ethical issues, you'd have gone to the police quietly months ago. You've obviously been collecting this information for a long, long time. You waited until now to release it because now is when it will hurt and humiliate Adam most."

"I knew you wouldn't understand." He began pleating his bed sheet in agitation just as he had the first time we talked about Cathleen.

"You're right. I don't. I guess I can accept that you could use me to help accomplish your schemes, even endangering my life—"

"I never meant to do that!" he said quickly, but I kept on.

"—but I can't understand what you did to Cathleen and Doris! Explain to me how you could tarnish Cathleen's memory before the world, how you could parade your defenseless wife in public!"

He looked at me, his eyes cold, his lips pinched together with anger. "You don't have any acquaintance with hate, do you?"

He was right. I didn't.

"Remember the day Bill Bozner came to visit you?" I asked.

Mr. Geohagan nodded.

"You lied to him. You said he could trust you."

"No lie." His voice was full of virtue. "He could trust me to do exactly what I did."

I shook my head in amazement. How he had convinced himself that he was guiltless!

"Why did Bozner even think at that point that maybe he should distrust you?"

The old man grinned. "They had never once suspected that for years I've been saving every evidence of Adam's financial indiscretion and wrongdoing I could get my hands on."

"Right," I said dryly. "You're the King of Duplicity. But how did you ever have access to that information?"

"I was comptroller for Hurlbert Construction from its beginning, Kristie. Didn't you know?"

I looked at him. "Comptroller?" I thought of the apartment and the garage. They certainly didn't indicate a man with a position of that importance and the salary that went with it. I wondered about the house he had sold, the one he had shared with Doris and Cathleen, the one I had never seen. "All I knew was that you worked for him. I assumed in construction itself."

"Not me," he said. "I'm a CPA, a Wharton School graduate. I've been on the inside of Hurlbert Construction from the get go. I've always known exactly where the company stood financially, where *he* stood financially. Oh, I never cared that Adam was taking kickbacks or evading his tax payments. Everyone does that. But if he ever got caught, as the company's CFO *I* was vulnerable. I was just making certain I wasn't going to be his scapegoat or get taken down with him."

"Even back then?"

"Always. Or at least from the beginning of his dishonesty anyway. He was straight at first. The greed kicked in later."

"But how'd they know to be distrustful of you now, after all those years?"

"The letters you sent them." He looked at me with great satisfaction.

"The letters I sent them?"

He was downright gleeful. "You mailed them for me! The first said *I know all about you!* and the second said *Think no one knows about your financial secrets? Just wait!*"

I stared at him. I remembered the letters. They'd been in his shirt pocket that day in the ER. He'd given me the first to mail the first time I visited, and I mailed the second on my way to spend the night in his closet. And I'd teased him about contributions!

"Did you always hate Adam so?"

He shook his head. "As a matter of fact, I used to like him. Oh, I've distrusted him for years. That's why I began keeping my private set of books. But he's a charming man. Funny. Clever. And I never expected to use my information. I didn't want to hurt him, just protect myself if the need ever arose. Turn state's witness. Plea bargain. That kind of thing. And that's the way it probably would have remained if he hadn't killed Cathleen!"

"Mr. Geohagan! *She* made that choice."

"He did! And he crippled Doris and ruined my life! He took away everything I've ever valued. Well, I'll just take him to hell with me."

The implacability of the obsessed, I thought as he struggled to breathe. I patted his hand to calm him.

"Why wasn't I supposed to tell anyone I had your key?" I finally asked.

"Because I didn't want one of those strange coincidences that can stalk life to ruin my plan. What if you had by some chance known Adam? A lot of people do. You might have unintentionally messed things up."

I shook my head in amazement. "You really had it planned, didn't you?"

Mr. Geohagan looked at me. "Don't judge me, Kristie. You're not the issue here. Neither are Cathleen or Doris. Adam is. He deserves everything that's going to happen to him! Look what he did to Cathleen, to Doris, to me! He ruined my life!"

I leaned forward. "Shh! Calm down. It's not good for you to get so upset."

He snorted. "You think I care?"

"I care." I was surprised to find I meant it. "I want you to get better. I want you to let go of your hate and bitterness. It's making you sicker than your physical problems. God can help you forgive and recover."

"No! I don't want to forgive and recover!" He was shaking with emotion. "No! Not God! Adam!"

I felt unbearable sorrow as I understood that he had chosen revenge and hatred over God.

"Shh," I said around the choking knot of emotion in my throat. "Be easy."

The door banged wildly against the wall, making us both jump, and in flew a Fury named Irene Parsons Carmody Hurlbert. Her hair was unkempt, and her face, without its usual masterful makeup, was blotched and pasty. Her jaw jutted forward, and her eyes flashed fire.

She strode to the bed and stood across from me, staring down at Everett Geohagan. Her face was ugly with loathing.

"How did you get in here?" I asked. "What do you want?"

She ignored me. All her energy was focused on Mr. Geohagan.

"You cruel old man! You foul, filthy beast! How dare you!" Venom dripped from each carefully enunciated word.

Mr. Geohagan shrank into his pillow, his face losing what little color it had.

"Stop that!" I reached across the bed and grabbed awkwardly

at Irene's wrist. "Leave him alone!"

She shook me off and grabbed Mr. Geohagan's shoulders, digging long, perfectly manicured talons into his frail body.

"How long have you been planning this, you evil creature? Ever since Adam left your sniveling daughter? Well, don't think we'll let you rip us apart without tearing you open too!" She shook his shoulders. "We'll take you down with us, I promise!"

"Let him go!" I grabbed Irene's hands, trying to pry them from Mr. Geohagan. She was so consumed by her hatred that I had all the impact of a fly.

"We'll make sure the world knows Cathleen was nothing but a common whore," Irene spat. "And you're no better, keeping your information for years and then selling it for a tidy profit!"

I jerked with surprise, finally drawing Irene's attention and scorn.

"You didn't actually believe his sanctimonious lies about protecting the people, did you?"

"Well, no," I said weakly. "But money?" I looked at him in dismay, and he stared stonily back. While I hadn't been naive enough to believe his stated rationale, I'd never imagined he'd been paid for his betrayal.

Irene laughed, sounding just like the evil queen in *Snow White*. Then she turned from me back to Mr. Geohagan.

"I'll get you, old man," she said. "You can depend on it." She reached for him again, grabbing a wrist and squeezing, squeezing. "You'll know the taste of gall, and you'll hurt like you didn't know you could hurt." She leaned over and hissed in his face like Cleopatra's asp. "You're a dead man."

"Stop it!" I yelled, running around the bed. "You're going to kill him!"

"Yes!" she yelled. "Good!"

I wrapped my arms around her waist, pulling her, dragging her back from the bed. "Help!" I screamed. "Help!"

It took all my strength to pull the woman away, so great was her fury. We stood locked together, my face buried in her back, while she fought to get free, then slowly, slowly calmed, slowly began to breathe more evenly.

"I'm okay," she finally spat out. "Just let me go!"

I had just released her when a nurse and an aide arrived in belated response to my screams. The nurse gasped at what she saw.

Irene and I looked with her at the bed. Irene smiled. Then she turned and calmly walked out.

"Out!" the nurse screamed at me as I stood frozen. She leaped astride Mr. Geohagan and began the first movement of the Resuscitation Ballet. "Crash cart!" she yelled at the aide who was already running.

I stood alone in the hall and watched the personnel and machines pour into Mr. Geohagan's room. I watched alone as the same people walked defeated from the room, wheeling the machinery before them. I cried alone as the nurse walked up to me and said, "I'm sorry."

TWENTY

I found myself in the woods, sitting beside the little pond I had painted not too long ago. The brilliant leaves were now gone from its surface, and the surrounding oaks, poplars, and maples were drained of color, the few clinging leaves brown and shriveled. But the burble of the tumbling water was somehow comforting, its gurgling music soothing.

I watched a bubble detach itself from the froth of the little waterfall and float in circles on the pool's surface. Suddenly it burst, gone, never to be seen again.

Like Mr. Geohagan.

I'd slept little last night, his voice with its various shadings and emotions running over and over through my mind.

Did I ever tell you that you remind me of my daughter, Cathleen?

You can't trust men who go to church, Kristie. They're too dumb to know what a wonderful woman you are.

I spent the last couple of days worrying about you. First there was that louse, What's-his-name, and then those men. Are you really all right?

You don't have any acquaintance with hate, do you?

No! Not God! Adam!

I rested my head on my knees and let a fresh wash of tears wet my jeans. I hadn't cried over Clarke, maybe because the hurt went so deep, but the absolute finality of Mr. Geohagan's rejection of God and the unalterable reality of his death undid what little emotional restraint I had left.

The Zooks had been so kind to me, so solicitous. Mary had hugged me and John had prayed with me—in High German—asking God to ease my heart's hurt. Even though I hadn't understood the words, I understood the tone, felt the concern.

And Jake. Early this morning he'd been in the great room as I tried to force myself to eat, and he'd taken my hand in his.

"I'm sorry, Kristie," he said. "I know how much the old man meant to you. I'm sorry he died and—" he swallowed hard—"and I'm sorry for everything else." He smiled awkwardly and turned bright red. "Uh, I'm going to my first GED class Monday."

I smiled weakly. "Good," I whispered. "I'm glad."

Then I went outside and walked and walked, trying to come to terms with Mr. Geohagan as the complex and all too human man that he was. Encourager and destroyer. Kindly friend and implacable enemy. Lover of family and hater of any who harmed them. My cheerleader and my manipulator.

I finally came to the patch of woods with the pond and sank onto my stone. So much had happened in so little time! My head and heart swam.

Monday I had had the discussion with Jake about hiding behind his family's faith. Judging by his kindness this morning, he had finally forgiven me.

Tuesday Clarke had come to my rescue—and left to fly home with Mary Ann.

Wednesday Barnum Hadley had showed up.

Thursday Ruth got married and Adam's perfidy was revealed.

Friday Cathleen's involvement with Adam became common knowledge, Mr. Geohagan made the absolute choice to hate instead of to know God, and Irene got her supreme revenge.

No wonder I was weary beyond concentration.

Oh, God, at least you're always there and always dependable.

I don't know how long I sat staring at the bubbling water as it leaped fearlessly over the edge of its falls, joyously seeking what came next, singing as it went. I decided that I wasn't up to leaping and singing yet, certainly not up to being joyous. I wouldn't be for some time. But I wanted—I needed—to move on with God.

Whatever waits ahead, God, I want to go through it with you. I choose you. I choose your way.

Both the silence of the woods and the babbling of the brook seemed confirmation from God that we had a pact. We sat quietly together.

Suddenly the woods were full of the sound of someone charging ahead, twigs snapping, leaves crackling. I jumped to my feet, back in the unpleasant and fearful memories of the man who had unnerved me here before.

"Kristie!" called the man, thrashing his way in my direction. *Clarke.* He began to run, and my heart began to pound. I managed to take a step or two before he reached me, but that was it. He grabbed me with an intensity and ferocity that undid me. I began to wail.

"Shh," he whispered. "Don't cry. It'll be all right. I'm never leaving you again. Never. Oh, Kristie, I'm so sorry I wasn't here with you when you needed me!"

Then I really cried, soaking the front of his jacket.

"He never believed," I sobbed. "He chose to hate."

"Some people do," he said, stroking my hair. "God doesn't force us to trust in him. Jesus may have died for the world, but the world doesn't all believe. For his own reasons, God allows that."

"But it's so sad!" I said. "It's bad enough to have him die, but to have him die in unbelief breaks my heart."

And he held me as I snuffled some more. Finally I pulled back and we both stared at the huge wet spot on the front of his jacket.

"It's supposed to be waterproof," he said in a disillusioned voice.

"You should never believe advertising claims," I hiccuped, running a shaky hand over my eyes, wiping away my tears. At least I hadn't put on mascara, so I didn't look like a raccoon. Just red rimmed. Very red rimmed. And blotchy.

"Now tell me, guy," I said, trying to sound at least a tad self-possessed. "What are you doing here? Where did you come from?"

"Where did you go?" he countered. "No, scratch that. You don't have to answer. I know."

"What do you know?" I asked. "I don't know anything!" The last was a wail. "I thought you were gone for good, off with the fair Mary Ann."

He looked at me quizzically. "We just went home to visit Mom and Dad. Mary Ann's been on the road for a year, so it was a family reunion of sorts. My only regret was that I couldn't take you along too."

Mom and Dad? Family reunion? I looked at him through narrowed eyes. "Just who is Mary Ann?"

"She's my younger and only sister." Then he began to laugh, having a wonderful time at my expense. "You thought..." He couldn't finish the sentence, he was laughing so hard.

I stood as straight as I could and stared haughtily at him. "If you'll think back, you never introduced me. All I know is that she kissed you in the church parking lot last Sunday and that you and she flew off together Tuesday night. And you never contacted me after she appeared. Not once." My voice wavered.

"Poor baby," he said, cupping my cheek.

I paused, then blurted, "Not that you contacted me much before she appeared either. If I hadn't been beaten up so many times, I'd probably never have seen you."

He looked at me, his smile still wide. He did have a beautiful smile. "I've just been waiting to see if Todd was truly a thing of the past," he said. "Do you know, I fell for you the first time I saw you, holding your cheek, your beautiful face all white and scared. Then you looked at me as we waited in the hospital and said in a haughty, don't-mess-with-me voice, 'I was just trying to make decent conversation.'"

"I did not!"

He nodded. "You did, sweetheart. I recognized you as a woman of spunk even then."

"Spunk! You like me because I've got spunk?" I was appalled. Where was the romance? The appreciation of all my finer qualities?

"No," he said. "I don't like you because you have spunk. I love you because you have spunk. And a kind heart. And a godly spirit. And the cutest red nose." He bent and kissed it, then hugged me again.

"I love you, too," I whispered into his shoulder. "I died a little each day when I thought you were gone forever." My arms tightened around him. "Don't leave me again, okay?"

Clarke tilted my chin. "Never," he said. "I promise." And he kissed me.

Some time later, we sat together on my rock, his arm around my shoulders, my arms wrapped around his waist.

Clarke tilted my chin. "About my sister. Mary Ann showed up unexpectedly Sunday morning. She sings with a Christian contemporary group, and they were driving from southern New Jersey to Harrisburg for an afternoon concert. They dropped her off on the way through, and I drove her to

Harrisburg. I didn't even know she was due in the area, or I'd have made sure I took you to hear her sing. She's got a wonderful voice."

I had an intense, though short, mental struggle recasting Mary Ann from the wicked-woman-who-stole-my-man to Clarke's sister. Too bad I'd been so distressed I'd never noticed her double name. Jon Clarke. Aunt Betty Lou. Mary Ann.

I shook my head. Nah. I'd never have picked up something so subtle even on a good day. Not with my penchant for jumping to conclusions.

Clarke continued his explanation, an explanation I was prepared to believe no matter how weak. But it wasn't weak, just a jumble of human confusion.

"I looked for you Sunday morning to take you to Harrisburg with us, but I didn't see you."

"I was in kindergarten church. I got an emergency call Saturday night and covered for a woman with a sick child."

He made a face. "All I knew was that I couldn't find you before or after the service, and Mary Ann kept saying that we had to go because she couldn't be late. Then she had a couple days off, and she stayed with Aunt Betty Lou and Uncle Bud until Tuesday evening when we went home. I wanted you two to get to know each other, so I called Monday evening as soon as I got home from work, but Jake said you weren't there. He said he'd give you my message."

"You called Monday night?"

"I also called Tuesday as soon as I thought you'd be home from school. When I said I had to leave town and absolutely must see you before I left, Jake said he didn't know where you were. Finally when we left for the airport, we stopped at Zooks'. Mary told me you were at the storage garage."

"You called Tuesday?"

"And Wednesday and Thursday and Friday. Several times."

"And Wednesday and Thursday and Friday? Several times?"

Clarke took me by the shoulders and gently shook me. "Do you always repeat what people say? You've got to get your own phone again, you know."

Clarke had called! He had tried to reach me! Not once but often!

"I didn't know you called," I said. "Jake never told me. He was mad at me."

Clarke nodded. "I know. Really mad. That's why he didn't mention the first couple of calls. Then he got too embarrassed to tell. But when you came home last night and told him about Mr. Geohagan, he knew he had to contact me and confess."

"He called you? That's why you're here? Why didn't he tell me?"

"He's afraid you're going to beat him up."

"Not a bad idea. The last few days have been horrible!"

Strong arms can make horrible memories less haunting.

"Anyway," Clarke said, "Jake called me. I've been on the phone, at the airport, in the air, and on the road for hours."

I noticed for the first time how weary he looked. "All for me?"

"All, my sweetestheart, for you."

Now that was romantic.

Dear Reader,

I first met Shirley Eaby (to whom this book is dedicated) about twenty-five years ago when we both began attending the St. Davids Christian Writers Conference. We clicked from the start and developed a strong and enduring friendship built on our mutual love for the Lord, our passion for writing, and our respect for each other.

We traveled to California and Florida to attend writers conferences together, began a writers critique group that met monthly at Shirley's house, and became director and assistant director of the Sandy Cove Christian Writers Conference in Maryland.

Through all these years we wrote and wrote, long projects, short projects, juvenile and adult projects. Some of our work was published, some not. Once when Shirley and I were commiserating about our lack of sales numbers, we looked at each other in mock horror and said, "What if God calls us to be encouragers of writers instead of much-published, popular writers ourselves!" For two ambitious women, this idea was a hard one to swallow.

The last time I visited Shirley, I took along my manuscript then in progress, a humor novel called *Enough!* Though Shirley was weak and obviously close to death, I decided to treat my visit with her as if it were a critique session. So as Shirley lay in her bed, I read a chapter to her. Once I thought she had fallen asleep on me and stopped reading. She opened her eyes and asked, "Why'd you stop?"

I resumed reading and she again closed her eyes. When I finished, she lay there for a few minutes. Then she said in her weak, barely audible voice, "You have two themes to your writing. Frustration and mystery."

Nonwriters may not understand what a wonderful memory

this last visit was for me, but as I kissed Shirley good-bye until eternity, I could only thank God for allowing the many years of friendship we enjoyed.

Now as I drive through Intercourse and Bird-in-Hand each month to Writers Arena, I miss Shirley's presence. I miss her friendship and her wise critiques. I miss her humor and her integrity. Most of all, I miss her loving encouragement.

Gayle Roper

Write to Gayle Roper
c/o Palisades
P.O. Box 1720
Sisters, Oregon 97759

THE PALISADES LINE

Look for these new releases at your local bookstore. If the title you seek is not in stock, the store may order you a copy using the ISBN listed.

Heartland Skies, Melody Carlson
ISBN 1-57673-264-9

Jayne Morgan moves to the small town of Paradise with the prospect of marriage, a new job, and plenty of horses to ride. But when her fiancé dumps her, she's left with loose ends. Then she wins a horse in a raffle, and the handsome rancher who boards her horse makes things look decidedly better.

Memories, Peggy Darty (May 1998)
ISBN 1-57673-171-5

In this sequel to *Promises,* Elizabeth Calloway is left with amnesia after witnessing a hit-and-run accident. Her husband, Michael, takes her on a vacation to Cancún so that she can relax and recover her memory. What they don't realize is that the killer is following them, hoping to wipe out Elizabeth's memory permanently....

Remembering the Roses, Marion Duckworth (June 1998)
ISBN 1-57673-236-3

Sammie Sternberg is trying to escape her memories of the man who betrayed her, and she ends up in a small town on the Olympic Peninsula in Washington. There she opens her dream business—an antique shop in an old Victorian—and meets a reclusive watercolor artist who helps to heal her broken heart.

Waterfalls, Robin Jones Gunn
ISBN 1-57673-221-5

In a visit to Glenbrooke, Oregon, Meredith Graham meets movie star Jacob Wilde and is sure he's the one. But when Meri puts her foot in her mouth, things fall apart. Is isn't until the two of them get thrown together working on a book-and-movie project that Jacob realizes his true feelings, and this time he's the one who's starstruck.

China Doll, Barbara Jean Hicks (June 1998)
ISBN 1-57673-262-2
Bronson Bailey is having a mid-life crisis: after years of globetrotting in his journalism career, he's feeling restless. Georgine Nichols has also reached a turning point: after years of longing for a child, she's decided to adopt. The problem is, now she's fallen in love with Bronson, and he doesn't want a child.

Angel in the Senate, Kristen Johnson Ingram
ISBN 1-57673-263-0
Newly elected senator Megan Likely heads to Washington with high hopes for making a difference in government. But accusations of election fraud, two shocking murders, and threats on her life make the Senate take a backseat. She needs to find answers, but she's not sure who she can trust anymore.

Irish Rogue, Annie Jones
ISBN 1-57673-189-8
Michael Shaughnessy has paid the price for stealing a pot of gold, and now he's ready to make amends to the people he's hurt. Fiona O'Dea is number one on his list. The problem is, Fiona doesn't want to let Michael near enough to hurt her again. But before she knows it, he's taken his Irish charm and worked his way back into her life...and her heart.

Forgotten, Lorena McCourtney
ISBN 1-57673-222-3
A woman wakes up in an Oregon hospital with no memory of who she is. When she's identified as Kat Cavanaugh, she returns

to her home in California. As Kat struggles to recover her memory, she meets a fiancé she doesn't trust and an attractive neighbor who can't believe how she's changed. She begins to wonder if she's really Kat Cavanaugh, but if she isn't, what happened to the real Kat?

The Key, Gayle Roper
ISBN 1-57673-223-1
On Kristie Matthews's first day living on an Amish farm, she gets bitten by a dog and is rushed to the emergency room by a handsome stranger. In the ER, an elderly man in the throes of a heart attack hands her a key and tells her to keep it safe. Suddenly odd accidents begin to happen to her, but no one's giving her any answers.

— ANTHOLOGIES —

Fools for Love, Ball, Brooks, Jones
ISBN 1-57673-235-5
By Karen Ball: Kitty starts pet-sitting, but when her clients turn out to be more than she can handle, she enlists help from a handsome handyman.
By Jennifer Brooks: Caleb Murphy tries to acquire a book collection from a widow, but she has one condition: he must marry her granddaughter first.
By Annie Jones: A college professor who has been burned by love vows not to be fooled twice, until her ex-fiancé shows up and ruins her plans!

Heart's Delight, Ball, Hicks, Noble
ISBN 1-57673-220-7
By Karen Ball: Corie receives a Valentine's Day date from her sisters and thinks she's finally found the one...until she learns she went out with the wrong man.

By Barbara Jean Hicks: Carina and Reid are determined to break up their parents' romance, but when it looks like things are working, they have a change of heart.

By Diane Noble: Two elderly bird-watchers set aside their differences to try to save a park from disaster but learn they've bitten off more than they can chew.

BE SURE TO LOOK FOR ANY OF THE 1997 TITLES
YOU MAY HAVE MISSED:

Surrender, **Lynn Bulock** (ISBN 1-57673-104-9)
Single mom Cassie Neel accepts a blind date from her children for her birthday.

Wise Man's House, **Melody Carlson** (ISBN 1-57673-070-0)
A young widow buys her childhood dream house, and a mysterious stranger moves into her caretaker's cottage.

Moonglow, **Peggy Darty** (ISBN 1-57673-112-X)
Tracy Kosell comes back to Moonglow, Georgia, and investigates a case with a former schoolmate, who's now a detective.

Promises, **Peggy Darty** (ISBN 1-57673-149-9)
A Christian psychologist asks her detective husband to help her find a dangerous woman.

Texas Tender, **Sharon Gillenwater** (ISBN 1-57673-111-1)
Shelby Nolan inherits a watermelon farm and asks the sheriff for help when two elderly men begin digging holes in her fields.

Clouds, **Robin Jones Gunn** (ISBN 1-57673-113-8)
Flight attendant Shelly Graham runs into her old boyfriend, Jonathan Renfield, and learns he's engaged.

Sunsets, **Robin Jones Gunn** (ISBN 1-57673-103-0)
Alissa Benson has a run-in at work with Brad Phillips, and is more than a little upset when she finds out he's her neighbor!

Snow Swan, **Barbara Jean Hicks** (ISBN 1-57673-107-3)
Toni, an unwed mother and a recovering alcoholic, falls in love for the first time. But if Clark finds out the truth about her past, will he still love her?

Irish Eyes, **Annie Jones** (ISBN 1-57673-108-1)
Julia Reed gets drawn into a crime involving a pot of gold and has her life turned upside down by Interpol agent Cameron O'Dea.

Father by Faith, **Annie Jones** (ISBN 1-57673-117-0)
Nina Jackson buys a dude ranch and hires cowboy Clint Cooper as her foreman, but her son, Alex, thinks Clint is his new daddy!

Stardust, **Shari MacDonald** (ISBN 1-57673-109-X)
Gillian Spencer gets her dream assignment but is shocked to learn she must work with Maxwell Bishop, who once broke her heart.

Kingdom Come, **Amanda MacLean** (ISBN 1-57673-120-0)
Ivy Rose Clayborne, M.D., pairs up with the grandson of the coal baron to fight the mining company that is ravaging her town.

Dear Silver, **Lorena McCourtney** (ISBN 1-57673-110-3)
When Silver Sinclair receives a letter from Chris Bentley ending their relationship, she's shocked, since she's never met the man!

Enough! **Gayle Roper** (ISBN 1-57673-185-5)
When Molly Gregory gets fed up with her three teenaged children, she announces that she's going on strike.

A Mother's Love, **Bergren, Colson, MacLean**
(ISBN 1-57673-106-5)
Three heartwarming stories share the joy of a mother's love.

Silver Bells, **Bergren, Krause, MacDonald**
(ISBN 1-57673-119-7)
Three novellas focus on romance during Christmastime.